How to Measure
Anything
Workbook

How to Measure Anything Workbook

Finding the Value of "Intangibles" in Business

DOUGLAS W. HUBBARD

WILEY

Contents

Preface

To Readers and Instructors,

This is the companion workbook for *How to Measure Anything: Finding the Value of Intangibles in Business*. While the book itself is not written as a textbook for universities, this workbook should help make the book a good text for a course in statistics or measurement. Like most workbooks, not every statement or argument in the book is covered—but the reader who has read and understood the material should do well with these questions.

This workbook is new with the third edition of *HTMA* (so be sure the correct edition is being used). The workbook covers each chapter of the book in order. The questions tend to focus on multiple choice, true/false, definitions, and calculations. Depending on the level of the course and the assumed background of the students, instructors may want to assign to the class projects involving the construction of more elaborate spreadsheet solutions. Otherwise, use of the prepared "power tools" provided on the website at www.howtomeasureanything.com may be sufficient for some courses. For a more challenging option, instructors can always ask students to develop some of those same power tools themselves.

Additional material specifically for instructors can be found at www.wiley.com. I believe the best exercises come from hands-on experience with team projects. Some suggestions for these projects are provided in the instructor materials but any difficult decisional analysis or measurement problem can be addressed with the methods covered in *HTMA*.

While the book was already being used in some university courses, this workbook and instructor materials will make it more widely adopted in higher education. Dealing with decisions under uncertainty and managing difficult measurements will be part of almost any modern career path after college, especially for those who successfully progress into upper management in industry or government. By reaching people before they enter the workforce, my hope is that some of the misconceptions this book discusses can be addressed early. Eventually, some of those students will get to positions where they will see firsthand some of the problems this book describes. Hopefully, some of those former students will be in a position to solve major problems in business and society at large with a little help from the quantitative methods I try to teach.

Thanks again to all readers who through their growing demand made a third edition feasible. And special thanks to the early adopters among the previous professors who looked at a book written for general management and saw a teaching tool that should be introduced at a much more fundamental level in someone's career.

I give special thanks to my staff, especially Tom Verdier and Chris Maddy, who helped with question generation, proofing, and generally keeping the project on track.

Douglas W. Hubbard

About the Author

Doug Hubbard is the president and founder of Hubbard Decision Research and the inventor of the powerful Applied Information Economics (AIE) method. His first book, *How to Measure Anything: Finding the Value of "Intangibles" in Business* (John Wiley & Sons, 2007, ed., 2010, 3rd ed., 2014), has been one of the most successful business statistics books ever written. He also wrote *The Failure of Risk Management: Why It's Broken and How to Fix It* (John Wiley & Sons, 2009), and *Pulse: The New Science of Harnessing Internet Buzz to Track Threats and Opportunities* (John Wiley & Sons, 2011). He has sold over 75,000 copies of his books in five languages.

Doug Hubbard's career has focused on the application of AIE to solve current business issues facing today's corporations. Mr. Hubbard has completed over 80 risk/return analyses of large critical projects, investments, and other management decisions in the past 19 years. AIE is the practical application of several fields of quantitative analysis, including Bayesian analysis, Monte Carlo simulations, and many others. Mr. Hubbard's consulting experience totals more than 25 years and spans many industries, including insurance, banking, utilities, federal and state government, entertainment media, military logistics, pharmaceuticals, cyber security, and manufacturing.

In addition to his books, Mr. Hubbard has been published in *CIO Magazine, Information Week, DBMS Magazine, Architecture Boston, OR/MS Today,* and *Analytics Magazine.* His AIE methodology has received critical praise from The Gartner Group, The Giga Information Group, and Forrester Research. He is a popular speaker at IT metrics and economics conferences all over the world. Prior to specializing in Applied Information Economics, his experiences include data and process modeling at all levels as well as strategic planning and technical design of systems.

How to Measure Anything Workbook

PART I

Questions

CHAPTER 1

The Challenge of Intangibles

LEARNING OBJECTIVES

- Describe different definitions of intangibles.
- Explain why measurements matter.
- Explain the different reasons for measurements.
- Explain the purpose of a decision-oriented framework for measurement.
- Describe the key steps in the Applied Information Economics approach to measurement.
- Explain why we use "power tools" for measurement.
- Provide an outline to the remainder of the book.

CHAPTER OVERVIEW

Chapter 1 proposes that anything can be measured and explains why measurements are critical to business, government, and life, and it outlines the case for this in the book. In business, there is an unlimited array of so-called "intangibles" like management effectiveness, research productivity, and public image, each of which turns out to be measurable by methods that are simpler than the reader may think.

The book proposes a "decision-oriented" framework for measurement. It is preferable to use quantitative models over unaided subjective intuition. For each decision, there are many "micro-decisions" about what to measure.

A method called Applied Information Economics (AIE) is introduced as a universal approach to measurement problems. The complexities of measurement can be simplified with a "power tools" approach to statistics.

QUESTIONS

1. Two common understandings of the word "intangible" apply to things that can be measured but are not _____, and things that cannot be measured at all. One purpose of this text is to argue that the second type of intangible _____.
   A. Physically touchable; does not exist
   B. Physically touchable; is the best-working definition of the word
   C. Analyzed; does not exist
   D. Analyzed; is unavoidable to some degree
   E. None of the above

2. To which type of decisions does this book apply?
   A. Government policy
   B. Personal decisions
   C. Business planning
   D. All of the above

3. Which of the following is true of intangibles?
   A. They defy measurement entirely.
   B. The term is essentially a misnomer because anything is measurable.
   C. They have little direct impact on decisions.
   D. They are rarely measurable and relatively unpredictable.

4. Which of the following statements is true of "intangible" variables?
   A. One can measure the tangible effects of seemingly "intangible" variables; if a variable literally had no detectable effect, then it would not be relevant to any decision.
   B. The low-cost measurement of "intangible" variables usually requires the application of state-of-the-art statistical techniques.
   C. Immeasurable variables can only be assessed intuitively.
   D. The routine treatment of "intangible" variables as unimportant in prevalent decision models suggests the effect of allegedly "immeasurable" factors is, in most cases, negligible.
   E. None of the above

5. If you are trying to figure out how a specific measurement process should work, how should you use this book?
   A. Check for your specific problem in the index. If you find it, skip to that chapter. If you don't find it, that issue is not addressed.
   B. The book is purely theoretical and doesn't address specific measurement problems.
   C. The steps described in the book apply to any measurement problem and are presented sequentially by chapter. Read the whole book and apply the steps within.
   D. None of the above

6. Which purpose of measurement is emphasized the most in this book?
   A. Measurements for resale
   B. Measurements for curiosity or entertainment
   C. Measurements that support decisions
   D. None of the above

7. Why do managers need to have a method to analyze options for reducing uncertainty about decisions?
   A. There are so many possible things to measure.
   B. Only some measurements impact the outcome.
   C. Measurements can be costly and time-consuming.
   D. All of the above

8. Which of the following statements is true?
   A. The value of a measurement is a direct function of the cost to obtain it.
   B. Measurements can be done only on things with no uncertainty.
   C. If a thing is difficult to measure, it's probably not as important to a decision.
   D. The value of a measurement is partly a function of the uncertainty associated with that variable.

9. Why are decision makers in organizations often less informed than they could be?
   A. They presume that some things are totally immeasurable.

B. They use traditional statistical methods to describe an intangible quantity.

C. They don't rely enough on experience and expert opinion.

D. They don't isolate and eliminate all uncertainty.

10. What is/are example(s) of a "micro-decision" to which the author refers?

   A. Small, inconsequential investments

   B. Small corrections to projects

   C. The choice about what to measure about a decision and how much to measure it

   D. All of the above

11. Which of the following statements about quantitative models is false?

   A. They don't have uncertainty.

   B. They tend to be more reliable than intuition.

   C. Studies indicate that they perform better than human judgment alone.

   D. They help to optimize the reduction of uncertainty.

12. Which is a valid reason for wanting to measure something?

   A. Upper management has suggested that it's a good idea.

   B. It's easy to do.

   C. It ultimately informs a decision of some kind.

   D. Any uncertainty in a decision process can lead to catastrophic consequences.

13. While the author stresses that "anything can be measured," why does he *not* also say that everything *should* be measured?

   A. The second statement is practical only when applied to micro-decisions.

   B. The second statement is contrary to basic economic measurement principles.

   C. The second statement applies only to cheap measurements.

   D. The second statement applies only to an organization's "core values."

14. True or False: Those who work in business tend to employ careful measurement methods more often than those working in the physical sciences.
True
False

15. Which of the following are examples of "power tools" as described in the book?
A. Proofs based on probability axioms
B. Spreadsheets
C. Tables
D. A list of mathematical laws of statistics to memorize
E. All of the above
F. B and C

16. What is the purpose of "power tools" as described in the book?
A. To teach us how to mathematically derive fundamental principles of statistics
B. To take apart each problem and make sure we understand every detail of the process
C. To make statistics practical to a wider audience
D. To help us quickly look up formulas

17. How do most scientists handle statistical measurement problems required for research?
A. They use software to analyze data and they copy output to their research articles.
B. They have committed all the required equations to memory.
C. They can derive all required equations from fundamental axioms.
D. They hand their data over to PhD statisticians for analysis.

18. Which of the statements below best describes the purpose of this book?
A. It discusses all types of measurement problems specifically.
B. It provides a framework for measurement that can be applied to any problem.

    C. It specifically mentions a small number of areas in which measurement methods may apply.

    D. It tells us why we should refrain from measurement whenever possible.

19. The methods of the book won't apply to which of the following so-called "intangibles"?

    A. The chance of a given political party winning the White House

    B. Public image

    C. The productivity of research

    D. Management effectiveness

    E. None of the above

20. What are some of the common misconceptions about statistics?

21. Provide three examples of alleged intangibles, or items that many might consider to be immeasurable. Keep track of them as you study the book and propose ways to measure them.

22. What is the first step of the Applied Information Economics framework?

23. Within the Applied Information Economics framework, when do you know it's okay to stop measuring?

CHAPTER 2

An Intuitive Measurement Habit: Eratosthenes, Enrico, and Emily

LEARNING OBJECTIVES

- Explain how three "measurement mentors" solved what might seem like complex measurement problems.
- Explain what lessons these measurement mentors teach us about measurement in general.

CHAPTER OVERVIEW

Throughout human history, there have always been people who were able to come up with intuitive measurement solutions to challenging problems. Chapter 2 takes a look at three such individuals who can serve as role models for us. Using a couple of simple observations and some basic geometry, Eratosthenes made a surprisingly accurate estimate of the circumference of Earth in the second century B.C. Nobel Prize–winning physicist Enrico Fermi taught his students to estimate the number of piano tuners in Chicago, and once measured the energy of an atomic bomb explosion using confetti. Finally, Emily Rosa teaches us that we need not be scientists, mathematicians, or even high school graduates to make clever measurements—she used a simple experiment to debunk paranormal claims and got her work published at the age of nine.

QUESTIONS

1. Which of the following is true of Eratosthenes's measurement of Earth's circumference?
   A. It is an ideal example in which a simple measurement was made using readily available information.
   B. It would not qualify as a true measurement by today's standards.
   C. It required a basic insight about Newtonian mechanics.
   D. It demonstrated the effectiveness of controlled experimentation, sampling, and randomization.

2. It was many centuries after Eratosthenes estimated the circumference of Earth that more accurate measurements were taken. What does this demonstrate?
   A. The methods and technology for measuring distance have not improved over time.
   B. It is possible to make what might seem an impossible measurement by making a clever calculation on some simple observations.
   C. Too much analysis often results in making absurd conclusions.
   D. Your instincts are usually right concerning the value of measurements.

3. What was the approximate error of Eratosthenes's estimation of the Earth's circumference?
   A. 20%
   B. 11%
   C. 3%
   D. 1.2%

4. If you wanted to estimate the number of auto mechanics in Providence, Rhode Island, which smaller piece(s) of information might be helpful?
   A. The number of people who drive cars there
   B. The average number of times a car must be taken to a mechanic
   C. The average workload of an auto mechanic
   D. All of the above

5. True or False: A Fermi decomposition is a measurement because it is based on new observations.
   True
   False

6. What measurement lesson(s) can we take from Enrico Fermi?
   A. When faced with a difficult estimation problem, it helps to decompose the object in question.
   B. There were slightly over 6 million people living in Chicago in the 1940s.
   C. When faced with a difficult measurement problem, you should focus further on your current uncertainties.
   D. Even when you don't know an exact quantity, you usually know something about the quantity in question.
   E. A and D

7. What measurement lesson(s) can we take from Emily Rosa?
   A. Simple methods such as controlled experiment, sampling, and randomization are effective tools in making measurements.
   B. Useful methods of experimentation need not be complicated or expensive.
   C. Even "intangibles" like healing energy fields can be tested by observation.
   D. All of the above

8. True or False: If you flipped a coin 100 times and guessed heads each time, it is more likely than not that you would achieve better accuracy than the therapists did in Emily's study.
   True
   False

9. What did the examples of measurements done by Eratosthenes, Enrico, and Emily have in common?
   A. The computing of statistical error
   B. Use of experimental methods
   C. Use of tools that weren't technologically advanced for their time
   D. Use of simple observations or decompositions

     E. All of the above
     F. C and D

10. Which of the following is true about simple measurements?
     A. They aren't very useful due to the large degree of uncertainty that remains.
     B. The more exhaustive studies will not reduce uncertainty further.
     C. They might reduce uncertainty significantly with little effort.
     D. None of the above

11. True or False: Psychologists like Paul Meehl taught us about the high levels of accuracy of our subjective judgments compared to statistical methods.
     True
     False

12. What basic pieces of information did Eratosthenes realize could be used to estimate Earth's circumference?

13. Give two objections managers and decision makers often offer as reasons not to attempt a measurement.

14. What did the author suggest that Mitre Information Infrastructure (MII) do to determine whether they actually improved the quality of deliverables?

15. Imagine you are a management consultant who has been engaged to help a major insurance company determine whether it would be well advised to open a new branch in Portland, Maine. Using the summary data below, show your calculations and propose the best course of action for this insurance company.

    ● There are 76,157 cars in Portland, Maine.
    ● According to the Insurance Information Institute, the average automobile insurance annual premium in the state of Maine is $657.12.

- Assume that, since coverage is mandatory, nearly all cars have insurance when calculating the gross insurance revenue in Portland, Maine.
- The average agent commission rate is 15%.
- There are a total of 58 insurance agencies in town.
- The insurance company considers a threshold of $500,000 per year in average agency commissions as the minimum standard for a successful branch.

Should the company open a new branch in Portland, Maine, or is the market in that area already saturated?

16. You are considering opening your own local car wash business. Propose a decomposition that you would use in order to evaluate whether there is sufficient market space for such a business in your area.

17. Recall how Enrico Fermi helped his students to estimate the number of piano tuners in Chicago. Drawing inspiration from his technique (known as a Fermi decomposition), estimate the number of dentists in Dallas, Texas.

18. Earth is approximately spherical, and the sun is far enough away that rays of sunlight are approximately parallel as they hit Earth. Suppose that at noon on the same day, the sun is directly above in one city (no shadows are cast) while in another city 250 miles to the north, the sun casts shadows with an angle of 3.6 degrees (1/100th of an arc of a circle). What is a rough estimate of the circumference of Earth?

19. At the Trinity test site, what was Fermi trying to find out, and what did he use to estimate it?

20. **Challenge:** Inspired by Emily Rosa, you decide to devise an inexpensive experiment to investigate a claim that an executive search firm is making. It claims it could determine which employees would be better leaders based on a personality interview conducted by a trained specialist. Twenty employees and four trained specialists from the search firm agree to participate. There may be multiple "hard" ways to do this, but propose how you might investigate a simpler question that is required to support the claim.

CHAPTER 3

The Illusion of Intangibles: Why Immeasurables Aren't

LEARNING OBJECTIVES

- Name three common misconceptions behind the claim that something can't be measured.
- Give a practical definition of the word "measurement."
- Describe the different scales of measurement.
- Explain the Clarification Chain.
- Describe several proven measurement methods that can be used for a variety of issues that are often considered immeasurable.
- Explain the "Rule of Five" and the "Urn of Mystery" examples.
- Present four useful measurement assumptions.
- Explain three reasons offered why something *shouldn't* be measured and how to counter them.

CHAPTER OVERVIEW

Chapter 3 exposes three common misconceptions that lead people to believe that something can't be measured. In describing these, several concepts are introduced. A practical definition of measurement is given and different scales of measurement are explained. Methods for improving the definition of an alleged immeasurable are discussed along with a basic overview of methods based on random sampling of observations. Four productive assumptions are given that help to reduce concerns about the difficulty and practicality of using measurements to inform decisions.

The chapter also discusses three commonly given reasons why something shouldn't be measured. It is shown that only one of these, the economic objection, has any potential merit but even that is overused.

QUESTIONS

1. What is/are a reason(s) people tend to think something can't be measured?
   A. The object of measurement is poorly defined.
   B. There is a lack of understanding of measurement methods.
   C. The concept of measurement is misunderstood.
   D. All of the above

2. According to the author, what is the only legitimate objection to why a certain thing should not be measured?
   A. Ethical objection
   B. Objection to efficacy of statistics
   C. Conceptual objection
   D. Economic objection

3. What does the mnemonic COM refer to?
   A. Characteristic, observation, meaning
   B. Correlation, opportunity, mechanism
   C. Comprehensive, ordinal, mathematical
   D. Concept, object, methods

4. Of the following, which is the best working definition of "measurement"?
   A. A process that can be used to assign a specific quantity or value
   B. An observation that informs you of something you knew before
   C. An observation that quantitatively reduces uncertainty
   D. A way of comparing the values of two similar things

5. Of the following, which is a useful first question to ask when facing a measurement problem?
   A. What do you mean, exactly?

   B. How much will it cost?
   C. When can we start measuring it?
   D. Who can we get to help us measure it?
   E. Where can we find an excuse for not measuring it?

6. Mathematician and electronics engineer Claude Shannon conceptu-
   alizes "information" as _____.
   A. Impossible to define mathematically
   B. The amount of uncertainty reduction in a signal
   C. The direct and deliberate transfer of perfect knowledge between
   a sender and recipient
   D. Exact quantities having no uncertainty

7. Nominal measurements are _____ statements, whereas ordi-
   nal measurements give a sense of whether one value is _____
   another (but not by some specified amount).
   A. Inverse; converging with
   B. Inverse; identical to
   C. Set membership; more than
   D. Set membership; also a member of

8. Which of the following is an example of a nominal scale?
   A. Gender
   B. Height
   C. Weight
   D. School ranking
   E. Temperature

9. Considering the scale of measurement, how many one-star movies
   would you have to watch to get the same level of enjoyment as a
   four-star movie?
   A. 1
   B. 4
   C. 16 (4 squared)
   D. 256 (4 to the fourth power)
   E. None of the above, as ordinal values cannot be meaningfully added
   or multiplied.

10. What is a reason it often seems that something is impossible to measure?
    A. It hasn't been properly defined yet.
    B. The tools for measuring that thing do not exist.
    C. Nobody has ever succeeded at measuring it.
    D. It's something that simply cannot be quantified.

11. To clarify what needs to be measured to study an investment in, for example, IT security, one should ask which of the following questions?
    A. "What do you mean by IT security?" and "Why do you care?"
    B. "Is this a Bayesian or a frequentist interpretation of IT security?"
    C. "What are the immeasurable variables?" and "Are the values high, medium, or low?"
    D. "What is the rank order of the proposed measurements?" and "Is this a nominal or an ordinal measurement problem?"

12. Use a thought experiment to make something more tangible, such as "work/life balance" or "customer satisfaction."

13. "If it matters, then it is detectible. If it is detectible, then it can be detected as an amount or as a range. If it can be detected as an amount or a range, then it is measurable."

    These three components define the _____, which connects alleged intangibles to means of measurement.

14. True or False: The word "statistics" derives from the Latin *statisticum*, which literally means "quantitative study of the stars."
    True
    False

15. What does the work of Paul Meehl, Philip Tetlock, and others mentioned in the book suggest about expert prediction?
    A. Due to underconfidence, experts are usually unwilling to make predictions.
    B. Expert prediction is typically better than statistical models.

C. Statistical models and expert prediction are equally accurate.

D. Statistical models are usually superior to expert judgment.

16. True or False: Measurements conducted via small random samples will have the greatest impact when the current state of uncertainty is high.

True

False

17. True or False: A census is required to have sufficient certainty for most decisions involving employee opinions.

True

False

18. The "Rule of Five" allows us to estimate with 93.75% certainty that the _____ of a population is between the largest and smallest observed values in a sample of five.

A. Mode

B. Mean

C. Median

D. Variance

19. Suppose you have an urn full of red and green marbles. You know that the proportion of either color is uniformly distributed anywhere between 0% and 100%. You reach your arm in and, without looking, draw a marble at random. The marble you select is green. What is the probability that the majority of the marbles are green?

A. The probability cannot be determined.

B. 1%

C. 51%

D. 75%

E. 99.99%

20. What lesson(s) can we take from the "Rule of Five" and "Urn of Mystery" examples?

A. You shouldn't attempt to reduce uncertainty without a large sample.

B. There is little need to gather data if information is limited.

C. You can learn a surprising amount about a population from small samples.

D. All of the above

21. According to the book, which of the following is an assumption that contradicts more common but less productive assumptions?

A. The problem is not as unique as you think.

B. There is presently no data with which to work.

C. You are the first to measure it.

D. Each problem is unique.

22. A commonly held misconception is that the higher your uncertainty, the _____ you need to significantly reduce uncertainty.

A. More data

B. More precision

C. Less data

D. More calculations

23. What do the highest-value measurements have in common?

A. Low uncertainty and low cost of being wrong

B. High uncertainty and low cost of being wrong

C. Low uncertainty and high cost of being wrong

D. High uncertainty and high cost of being wrong

24. If the clinician in Paul Meehl's example were aware of the statistical risks of psychotic depression, what tragedy might have been avoided?

25. Using the clarification chain, walk through a possible way to measure customer satisfaction for a hotel. Provide a brief answer that leads to a single measurement you would recommend.

26. What is the Latin origin of the word *experiment*?

27. A manager intends to use the "Rule of Five" to determine which of a dozen different restaurants to hold the company holiday party in. Why won't this approach work?

28. Why must something be detectable in order for it to matter?

29. Give an example of an ethical objection to measurement and how you might refute it.

30. What is an example of the Uniqueness Fallacy?

31. Challenge: Compute the probabilities associated with a "Rule of X," where X is an integer going from 2 to 10. For each X, what is the probability that the median of a population would be somewhere between the smallest and largest values in a sample size of X?

32. Challenge: Write a brief editorial about a specific situation when, had a business or other organization used one or more of the four measurement assumptions presented in the chapter, better outcomes could have been achieved through either better accuracy or a savings of resources.

Clarifying the Measurement Problem

LEARNING OBJECTIVES

- Explain what needs to be addressed prior to making a measurement.
- Explain challenges and solutions for defining a decision.
- Explain the difference between "uncertainty" and "risk."
- Identify some of the issues organizations have with some of their initial attempts to measure what seems abstract, such as IT security or agricultural resilience.
- Describe how even seemingly abstract measurements can be defined in terms of the decisions they support and how to decompose them further.

CHAPTER OVERVIEW

Chapter 4 addresses questions that must be asked prior to making a measurement. Measurements are used to support decisions, and the thing being measured must be defined in terms of observable consequences that relate to your decision in a particular way. A key challenge is often how to define the relevant decision. The concepts of "uncertainty" and "risk" are often misunderstood, so a clear definition of the two is provided.

The Applied Information Economics process is described in more detail. IT security and agricultural sustainability are given as examples of decision identification, clarification, and decomposition. A major issue in these examples, as in many measurement problems, is that they were not initially defined in terms of observable consequences and decisions they support. After framing the problem in this way, it becomes possible to decompose it into a variety of more specific, measurable components.

QUESTIONS

1. Which of the following needs to be answered prior to making a measurement?
   A. What is the decision this measurement is supposed to support?
   B. What is the definition of the thing being measured in terms of observable consequences?
   C. How, exactly, does this thing matter to the decision being asked?
   D. All of the above

2. How can we determine whether or not a measurement has value?
   A. By asking management whether they consider the variable to be a critical one
   B. By validating that the outcome of the measurement will have an impact on some decision
   C. A measurement has value if it is included in a management report, whether or not that report is used to make decisions.
   D. All of the above

3. Which of the following represents the correct order of the Applied Information Economics framework?
   A. Define a decision problem and the relevant uncertainties; compute the value of additional information; make a decision and act on it; determine what you know now; apply the relevant measurement instrument(s) to high-value measurements.
   B. Determine what you know now; define a decision problem and the relevant uncertainties; apply the relevant measurement instrument(s) to high-value measurements; compute the value of additional information; make a decision and act on it.
   C. Determine what you know now; make a decision and act on it; define a decision problem and the relevant uncertainties; compute the value of additional information; apply the relevant measurement instrument(s) to high-value measurements.

    D. Define a decision problem and the relevant uncertainties; determine what you know now; compute the value of additional information; apply the relevant measurement instrument(s) to high-value measurements; make a decision and act on it.

4. Which of the following is/are requirement(s) for a decision?
   A. Uncertainty
   B. Potentially negative consequences
   C. No more than one realistic alternative
   D. All of the above

5. True or False: It is important to measure greenhouse gas emissions even if the knowledge couldn't be used to take a different course of action.
   True
   False

6. True or False: An unidentified decision is no better than having no decision in mind at all.
   True
   False

7. True or False: Human intuition can be a decision model.
   True
   False

8. Which of the following is true of a simple cost-benefit analysis?
   A. It is a model, but it's too simple to ever be of any practical use.
   B. It doesn't qualify as a decision model.
   C. Costs and benefits can be decomposed.
   D. It requires advanced knowledge of statistical theory.

9. True or False: Decomposing uncertain variables actually increases error for highly uncertain quantities.
   True
   False

10. MacGregor and Armstrong concluded which of the following about decomposition?
   A. It is most helpful when there is little uncertainty.
   B. It is appropriate for use under conditions of certainty only.
   C. It can reduce error for highly uncertain variables by a factor of 10 to 100.
   D. Decomposition alone has little impact unless coupled with additional empirical measurements.
   E. B and C

11. Which of the following is an example of a false dichotomy?
   A. A Monte Carlo simulation
   B. Trying to decide whether or not your company should have worker safety
   C. Deciding that there is between a 20% and 45% chance that a particular investment will not be profitable
   D. Choosing whether or not to develop a new product this year
   E. Choosing whether a particular investment in a safety program is justified

12. Which of the following is/are relevant question(s) for measuring "product quality"?
   A. What decision will it affect?
   B. What is meant by "product quality"?
   C. How can we eliminate uncertainty about this concept?
   D. All of the above
   E. A and B

13. True or False: If a company produces weekly reports that have no bearing on decisions of any kind, then their information value for decisions is zero.
   True
   False

14. True or False: There are no major industries that already attempt to measure uncertainty and risk.
   True
   False

15. Which of the following statements about risk and uncertainty is true?
   A. Both imply an outcome that is undesirable.
   B. Uncertainty is a type of risk, but risk is not a type of uncertainty.
   C. Both denote a lack of complete certainty.
   D. Neither can be quantified.

16. True or False: "Over the next five years, there is a 90% chance that this item will double in value and a 10% chance that its value will increase by 50%." This statement represents a measurement of risk.
   True
   False

17. True or False: The author believes that bureaucracies insulated from practical economic decisions exist in both government and corporations.
   True
   False

18. What is an advantage of modeling decisions quantitatively, rather than intuitively?
   A. Intuitive models are more inconsistent.
   B. Intuitive models contain more logical inference errors.
   C. Intuitive models contain more unstated assumptions.
   D. All of the above
   E. B and C

19. True or False: Frank Knight was the first person to define risk and uncertainty.
   True
   False

20. An improvement in "security" would imply which of the following?
   A. An increase in uncertainty
   B. An increase in the costs of security analysts
   C. An increase in the probability of loss
   D. A decrease in risk

21. What was a key problem in the way the VA initially dealt with IT security?
    A. They didn't focus enough on administrative measurements like the number of people who attended training.
    B. They didn't focus on the results of security breaches.
    C. They defined security in a measurable way.
    D. They used "Fermi questions" to decompose their problem.

22. Which of the following "Fermi questions" was/were asked to estimate the impact of virus attacks?
    A. How often does the average pandemic (agency-wide) virus attack occur?
    B. For the affected population, how much did their productivity decrease relative to normal levels?
    C. What is the cost of labor lost during the productivity loss?
    D. All of the above
    E. B and C

23. When asked to estimate the parameters of the effect of virus attacks, how were the amounts calculated?
    A. Precisely from extensive historical data.
    B. They gave a 90% confidence interval.
    C. Experts were asked to estimate single point values for each.
    D. They were asked to evaluate each as a high, medium, or low risk.

24. Explain why corporate "dashboards" might contain data that is not valuable.

25. When the author measured IT security for the VA, what were two or more examples of breaches of IT security?

26. Briefly describe the difference between "uncertainty" and "risk," according to the book.

27. The author compared examples from two very different fields—IT security and environmental sustainability. What do security in IT and environmental sustainability have in common?

28. Decisions vary by which of the following ways?
  A. Decisions may be continuous or discrete and may have one or many stakeholders.
  B. Decisions may be large, infrequent decisions or small, frequent operational decisions.
  C. Decisions may or may not involve uncertainty about negative consequences.
  D. A and B
  E. All of the above

CHAPTER 5

Calibrated Estimates: How Much Do You Know *Now?*

LEARNING OBJECTIVES

- Define the term "confidence interval" and explain its role in the AIE process.
- Describe two extremes of biases in subjective confidence.
- Evaluate your own ability to calibrate probabilities.
- Describe methods used to calibrate people.
- Explain some of the conceptual obstacles to accurate calibration.
- Describe the performance of individuals in calibration training research.

CHAPTER OVERVIEW

Chapter 5 explains how a person can describe one's own uncertainty quantitatively. Most research suggests that, due to things like overconfidence and underconfidence, people are not very good estimators of probability. However, there are ways to improve on this with training.

In these exercises, participants assess their confidence about a series of statements (either 90% confidence interval or binary true/false) and are then shown the correct answers, giving them immediate feedback showing whether their stated probabilities were realistic. A variety of other means for improving your calibration are also recommended, and further insight into the variation in individual performance is provided.

QUESTIONS

1. Suppose you are asked how many leads you expect will turn into sales, and you give a 90% confidence interval of 11 to 23. What does this mean?

    A. You have very little information about how many leads will turn into sales.

    B. You believe there is a 90% chance the actual number will be between 11 and 23.

    C. You are 90% sure the actual number will be outside the range of 11 and 23.

    D. You are certain the number will be between 9.9 and 20.7.

2. True or False: Suppose you give a 90% confidence interval of 0 to 30 bugs per lines of code in a software development project. This means that, on average, there are 15 bugs per line of code.

    True

    False

3. True or False: Probabilities can't be used to describe your uncertainty about future events.

    True

    False

4. What have the studies of Kahneman and Tversky indicated about the natural ability of individuals to come up with accurate probability estimates?

    A. Most people are very overconfident.

    B. Humans fairly realistically describe their uncertainty, even without practice.

    C. Most people are extremely underconfident.

    D. Humans are equally likely to be overconfident or underconfident.

5. According to the book, why might bookies be better estimators of probability than physicians?

    A. IQ determines who estimates probability accurately.

    B. Gamblers are overconfident in their ability to assess probabilities.

C. Doctors are underconfident in their ability to assess probabilities.

D. The estimation of probability is a learned skill.

6. In a calibration test, if you have maximum uncertainty (i.e., no idea) what an answer to a binary question is, approximately what is your chance of getting the answer correct?

7. True or False: If you are not calibrated, you have a greater chance of getting about 90% within your stated range if you take a 10-question calibration test than a 100-question calibration test.
   True
   False

8. True or False: Skill at trivia is essential to becoming a calibrated estimator.
   True
   False

9. From the choices below, select the one that best describes the likelihood that a calibrated person would correctly answer just six or fewer questions on a 10-question test.
   A. Less than a 2% chance
   B. Less than a 1 in 10 billion chance
   C. Greater than a 60% chance but less than a 90% chance
   D. Greater than a 99% chance

10. Suppose you are 75% sure of X. In the "equivalent bet" test you would verify this by comparing which of the following options?
    A. Win $1,000 if X is true OR take a certain $1,000 payment in cash.
    B. Be 75% confident OR take $1,000.
    C. Win $1,000 if X is true OR spin a dial that gives a 75% chance of paying $1,000.
    D. None of the above

11. Suppose your confidence in 10 calibration questions is: 0.5, 0.6, 0.7, 0.7, 0.5, 0.6, 0.6, 0.8, 1, 0.5. To score as closely as possible to being

perfectly calibrated on the test, how many of the items would you
end up getting correct?

A. This cannot be answered because none are known for certain.

B. Since only one answer is known for certain, only one is
expected to be correct.

C. Since 6.5 is the sum of the probabilities, getting six or seven
correct would be closest to the expected performance.

D. Since all are at least 0.5, you expect to get all 10 correct.

12. True or False: If a person is calibrated, there is less than a one in 500
chance that the person will get five or fewer answers within a set of
ten 90% confidence intervals.
True
False

13. Why did De Finetti refer to the probability of X as Pr(X) as opposed
to the more common P(X)?

A. He considered all probabilities to be *posterior probabilities*.

B. He wanted to equate *price* and *probability*.

C. He considered all probabilities to be *prior probabilities*.

D. He believed all probabilities to be *perfect probabilities*.

14. Which of the following has not been demonstrated to improve the
calibration of probabilities?

A. Coming up with answers quickly and intuitively

B. Practicing with multiple calibration tests

C. Pretending to bet on the outcome with the equivalent bet

D. Identifying reasons that an estimate might be wrong

15. Which of the following approaches is most helpful for curbing your
natural anchoring tendency?

A. Decide on a best estimate, or most likely value, and then impose
an interval around that value to account for error.

B. Start with an extremely wide range and then consider the two
bounds as separate calibration questions (i.e., you are 95% confident the answer is above the lower bound and 95% confident the
answer is below the upper bound).

C. Start with a narrow interval and widen it until the interval contains all reasonable values.

D. Pick a lower bound that reflects the lowest possible value you believe the variable might assume. Then, select an upper bound that reflects the maximum possible value you believe the variable might assume.

16. Which of the following objections to calibration questions indicate(s) a misunderstanding of subjective probability and why it is used?

   A. "This is my 90% confidence interval but I have absolutely no idea if it is right."

   B. "We couldn't possibly estimate this. We have no idea."

   C. "Why not just put a ridiculously wide range on everything? Then every range will be right."

   D. All of the above

17. True or False: If you give a 100% confidence interval when asked to give a 90% confidence interval, you are essentially expressing underconfidence.

   True

   False

18. True or False: Calibration training assumes that probability is an objective thing that is a property of the world outside of the human observer.

   True

   False

19. A member of which of the following schools of thought would argue that, during a calibration exercise, the correct answer either is or is not within a range and, therefore, a "probability" doesn't apply?

   A. A Bayesian

   B. A frequentist

   C. A subjectivist

   D. All of the above

20. Which of the following is true of frequentist interpretations of statistics?

   A. A probability is a type of idealized frequency.

B. Probabilities apply only to random, infinite, and strictly repeatable trials.

C. Probability is not simply a degree of belief of an individual.

D. All of the above

21. Which of the following is the main advantage of the author's research on calibration, relative to the academic research?
    A. It is more informative about the variations among individual performances.
    B. It is more informative about group average performance.
    C. It uses better calibration questions.

22. True or False: Proven performance in calibration training using trivia questions reflects an ability to assess the odds of real-life uncertainties.
    True
    False

23. Given that a person has completed their first calibration exercise consisting of range questions and that they have provided correct ranges for 9 out of the 10 total questions, _____.
    A. We can state with absolute certainty that they are calibrated
    B. They may be closer to being calibrated than most people, but it is still more likely that they are uncalibrated and lucky
    C. We cannot allow the results of a single test to influence our assessment of a person's level of calibration
    D. We can state with absolute certainty that this person is underconfident

24. In what responses on a true/false test is there no statistically allowable error at all?

25. Which of the following is/are valid conclusion(s) about the Giga study?
    A. Those who received calibration training performed better than those who didn't.

B. Those who didn't receive calibration training performed just as well.

C. The Giga analysts had a knowledge advantage regarding these questions.

D. All of the above

E. B and C

26. According to the author's observations, about what percentage of calibration training participants achieve calibration by the end of the training?

A. About 50%

B. About 95%

C. About 80%

D. About 25%

27. Explain why accurately quantifying your baseline level of uncertainty is an important step in the Applied Information Economics (AIE) process.

CHAPTER 6

Quantifying Risk through Modeling

LEARNING OBJECTIVES

- Describe some common problems with the way risk is usually measured.
- Describe the placebo effect in risk management.
- Describe the origins of the Monte Carlo simulation.
- Run a simple Monte Carlo simulation in Excel.
- Describe three frequency distributions and how each might be used in Monte Carlo simulations.
- Review some of the more advanced Monte Carlo concepts provided in the chapter.
- Define and give an example of the "risk paradox."

CHAPTER OVERVIEW

Risk is a foundation of other important measurements that support decisions, but is not assessed adequately in most organizations. The Monte Carlo simulation uses ranges to represent uncertainty rather than point values, and generates many possible scenarios that allow us to get a more realistic sense of the risks involved. These calculations are practical and can be accomplished with Microsoft Excel. An understanding of standard probability distributions, such as the normal and binary, is helpful. Other resources are provided, and future directions for "probability management" are outlined.

There is a tendency in business to use quantitative risk analysis for routine operational decisions only, while critical strategic decisions are left to inferior means of analysis. Research on use of Monte

Carlo tools has demonstrated that they improve a firm's overall financial performance. Recommendations for probability management are outlined.

QUESTIONS

1. True or False: According to the author, risk is often measured in ways that are ambiguous and don't address human bias.
   True
   False

2. Managers should spend less effort focusing on feeling good about decisions and more time doing which of the following?
   A. Measuring only what is certain
   B. Measuring evidence that decisions and forecasts have improved
   C. Developing any kind of method, even if it means using arbitrary weighted scores
   D. All of the above
   E. B and C

3. Which is not an advantage of the Monte Carlo simulation?
   A. It is a helpful tool for traditional accounting tasks.
   B. It can be performed on any modern personal computer.
   C. It helps determine return on investment when exact costs and benefits are unknown.
   D. It allows the user to compute the probabilities of various outcomes.

4. Which of the following is an example of the placebo effect in calculating risk?
   A. Using a system for measuring risk based on the feeling that it works without considering outcomes
   B. Measuring uncertainty about a particular benefit of using a product
   C. Using traditional accounting methods to measure precise variables
   D. Not using control groups for your experiments

5. A 90% confidence interval of a variable with a normal distribution is a range equal to the size of how many standard deviations?
   A. 1.3
   B. 3.29
   C. 10
   D. 900

6. In Microsoft Excel, which function can you use to look up how many of your results exceeded the breakeven level?
   A. Daverage
   B. Normsdist
   C. Countif
   D. Autosum

7. Consider the following risk in a construction project: In a given month, there is a 5% chance of a worksite accident that would cause losses of up to $10 million in work stoppage and liabilities. Suppose that we have reason to believe that the losses cannot exceed $10 million if an accident occurs, and assume that all possible loss amounts up to that maximum are equally likely. What is a correct way to model this loss in Excel?
   A. =if(rand()>.05,rand()*10000000,0)
   B. =if(rand()=.05,norminv(rand(),10000000,.05))
   C. =if(rand()<=.05,rand()*10000000,0)
   D. =if(rand()<.05,0,rand()*10000000)

8. In the previous construction project risk example, what is the chance that the loss will exceed $8 million?
   A. 1%
   B. 5%
   C. 7%
   D. None of the above

9. Suppose losses of up to $5,000,000 are insured in the previous example. Which of the following models the loss correctly?
   A. = if(rand()<$5000000, rand()*10000000,0)
   B. = if(rand()<0.05, MAX(RAND()*10000000 − 5000000,0), 0)
   C. = if(rand()<.05,if(rand()<.5,rand()*10000000,0))
   D. = if(rand()>.05,rand()*10000000-5000000,0)

10. Write the formula to generate a normally distributed variable with a 90% CI of 80 to 160.

11. True or False: The difference between the midpoint of the range and either of the bounds of a 90% confidence interval is also known as the standard deviation.
    True
    False

12. What type of distribution can be used for modeling the probability of a single event with two possible outcomes?
    A. Normal
    B. Beta
    C. Bernoulli
    D. Uniform

13. What type of distribution should you use to represent a variable that has a 100% chance of being between two bounds but is equally likely to take on any value between the bounds?
    A. Normal
    B. Beta
    C. Bernoulli
    D. Uniform

14. Suppose you are considering whether or not to fund a particular start-up. Calibrated estimators give a range of $1.1MM to $4.0MM for the cash you have to put into the business in Year 1, and they estimate the Year 1 revenue at $1.8MM to $4.8MM. In addition, there is a 50% chance that a grant with a value from $200,000 to $500,000

will be paid during Year 1. Assume all of these ranges are 90% CIs for normal distributions.

Losing more than $1MM on this project in the first year would be financially ruinous for your company. What is the chance of that happening?

A. 5.7%

B. 14.5%

C. 20.6%

D. 33.1%

15. Suppose you are a salesperson with two major new deals for this month. Prospect A has a 75% chance of closing and generating $1 million to $2 million in revenue. Prospect B has a 50% chance of closing and generating $1 million to $3 million in revenue. Each value in your revenue ranges has an equal chance of occurring. You've been behind on your quota, so your manager tells you that if you don't make at least $1.5 million this month, you will be fired. What is your chance of being fired?

16. You need to simulate a system in sequential steps where each step affects the probabilities of the following step. What type of simulation or model is this?

A. Simulation of correlations

B. Markov simulation

C. Agent-based model

D. All of the above

E. A and B

17. For each of the following, there are a pair of separate possible winnings. Which of the following pairs would a risk-neutral person consider equivalent to each other?

A. A 1% chance of winning $500 and a 50% chance of winning $1

B. A 1% chance of winning $100 and a 100% chance of winning $10

C. A 3% chance of winning $10,000 and a 30% chance of winning $1,000

D. All of the above

E. B and C

18. Which of the following is a challenge with using Monte Carlo simulations?

    A. They have to be built from scratch.

    B. They are meant to be understood only by statisticians.

    C. They require knowledge of computer programming.

    D. None of the above

19. Which of the following would be responsibilities of a chief probability officer (CPO)?

    A. Payroll accounting

    B. Managing a library of probability distributions

    C. Managing SIPS and SLURPS

    D. All of the above

    E. B and C

20. True or False: SLURPS are basically SIPS that account for the correlations between variables.

    True

    False

21. True or False: The popular author Nassim Taleb has been critical of the usage of Monte Carlo simulations in the financial industry.

    True

    False

22. Without using a Monte Carlo simulation, what is the 90% CI for the sum of two normally distributed values with 90% CIs of 20 to 40 and 30 to 60?

23. Explain what is problematic about this statement: "As far as I'm concerned, a low risk of losing $3 million is worse than a medium risk of losing $1 million."

24. Give at least two recommendations the author offers for probability management.

25. Explain the risk paradox, and give an example.

26. Name three Monte Carlo tools.

27. Challenge: Create a Monte Carlo simulation that models possible outcomes for the following situation. (This challenge problem will require a bit more understanding of features of Excel than is explicitly covered in the book, but it should be feasible for anyone experienced with data analysis in Excel.)

When there are no specific delays, the amount of time a blood and tissue delivery truck spends in transit between facilities follows approximately a normal distribution with a 90% confidence interval of 3.5 hours to 4.25 hours. Sometimes the delivery driver experiences an additional delay that adds time to the total transit time. By contract, the delivery vendor is not compensated for deliveries that arrive two hours late or more. Consider the weather and road construction as reasons for delay. Create a Monte Carlo simulation with 10,000 trials of delivery times and estimate the percentage of deliveries that are two hours late or more. In your simulation, suppose the following probabilities and 90% confidence intervals:

- The probability of the weather causing a delay is estimated to be 10%.
- The probability of road construction causing a delay is estimated to be 15%.
- If the weather does cause a delay, then add another 30 minutes to five hours to the baseline transit time (90% confidence interval and normal distribution).
- If road construction causes a delay, then add another five minutes to two hours to the baseline transit time (90% confidence interval on a uniform distribution).

Create a relative frequency table and a histogram to summarize the results of the Monte Carlo trials, and plot the results on a histogram. Owwne must select a lower and upper limit (here 2 has been chosen for the lower limit and 12 has been chosen as the upper limit), and an increment for the bin (here, an increment of 0.01 has been chosen).

Quantifying the Value of Information

LEARNING OBJECTIVES

- Explain Expected Opportunity Loss, and learn how it is calculated.
- Learn how to compute EVPI for ranges.
- Explain the difference between EVI and ECI curves and a practical implication.
- Define and give examples of a common "Measurement Myth."
- Define and give an example of "Measurement Inversion."
- Review definitions for "uncertainty," "risk," and "information value."

CHAPTER OVERVIEW

Chapter 7 focuses on how to compute the value of information for decisions and how this affects measurements. Expected Opportunity Loss (EOL) is a simple calculation of risk, which is equivalent to Expected Value of Perfect Information (EVPI). Discrete, binary outcomes have an easily computed EVPI. Uncertainties are frequently expressed as ranges and EVPI calculations for those situations are discussed. The book and website provide tools for calculating EVPI for ranges. While EVPI represents uncertainty elimination, uncertainty reduction is a more practical goal, so general considerations are provided for calculating values and costs of uncertainty reduction.

It is often thought that the more uncertainty you have, the more data you will need to reduce it, and this chapter describes why the exact opposite is in fact the case. In addition, more attention is incorrectly paid to measuring variables of lower economic value, a phenomenon the author refers to as "measurement inversion." These tendencies are seen across business sectors. The chapter closes with a summary of uncertainty, risk, and information value, as well as some important takeaway lessons from the book thus far.

QUESTIONS

1. If the value of information is derived through the impact it has on the behavior of others (not the person gathering the information), which of the following statements is true?
   A. In terms of human behavior, the value of information is equal to the value of the difference in behavior.
   B. It is impossible to put a value on human behavior.
   C. Due to human idiosyncrasies, the value of information is slightly less than the value of the difference in behavior.
   D. In terms of human behavior, the value of information is slightly higher than the value of the difference in behavior.

2. Which of the following statements is true?
   A. Loss functions must be linear.
   B. Loss functions may be bidirectional.
   C. Loss functions apply to uncertainties on a continuum but not decisions on a continuum.
   D. Whether or not to purchase a hotel based on uncertainties about future room occupancy is an example of a decision on a continuum with an uncertain binary variable to measure.

3. Which of the following describes an Expected Opportunity Loss in its simplest form?
   A. The sum of the "wrong" choice and the best alternative available
   B. The difference between the "right" choice and the best alternative available
   C. The cost of being "wrong" times the chance of being "wrong"
   D. The product of the "wrong" choice and the most readily available alternative

4. If a person is risk neutral they would:
   A. Prefer a certain cash payment of $100,000 to a 10% chance of winning $1 million
   B. Prefer a 10% chance of winning $1 million to a certain cash payment of $100,000
   C. Be indifferent between a 10% chance of winning $1 million and a certain cash payment of $100,000
   D. Prefer $50,000 cash to a 50% chance of winning $1 million

5. Which of the following define(s) the Expected Value of Information (EVI)?
   A. The value of the reduction in decision risk
   B. The expected difference between the EOL before and after a measurement
   C. The difference between the reduction in risk and the EOL after a measurement
   D. All of the above
   E. A and B

6. True or False: In the expected value of information calculation, an $EOL_{After\ Info}$ of 0 indicates perfect information was gathered.
   True
   False

7. Binary EOL calculations are _____ than those on a continuum, but they're also _____.
   A. More complicated; more realistic
   B. Simpler; less realistic
   C. Simpler; more realistic
   D. More complicated; less realistic

8. Define a "threshold" of an uncertain variable in a decision.

9. Suppose you are trying to determine whether to invest in a lease of a cutting-edge piece of machinery for your manufacturing firm at a cost of $3,000,000 over the cost of the lease for standard equipment.

Both leases have the same term of 12 months. Calibrated estimators give a 90% confidence interval between 300,000 and 800,000 extra units produced during the lease term, normally distributed. Given your gross margins, each product produced earns you $6 in profits. Which of the following values is closest to your Expected Value of Perfect Information (EVPI) for this potential measurement?

A. $240,000

B. $340,000

C. $440,000

D. $540,000

10. Which of the following is/are characteristic(s) of the EVI curve?

A. The rise in EVI is steepest during the initial uncertainty reduction.

B. The value of EVI can never exceed EVPI.

C. The EVI is always decreasing.

D. All of the above

E. A and B

11. Which of the following statements about the difference between EVPI and EVI is true?

A. EVI is more realistic because it applies to reduction rather than elimination of uncertainty, but EVPI is more easily calculated.

B. EVPI is more realistic because it applies to reduction rather than elimination of uncertainty, but EVI is more easily calculated.

C. EVI can be applied only to problems with normal probability distributions.

D. EVPI can be applied only to problems with normal probability distributions.

12. The curvature of the EVI indicates that if you can reduce uncertainty by half in a measurement, the EVI is equal to:

A. Less than half of the EVPI

B. More than half of the ECI

C. Less than half of the ECI

D. More than half of the EVPI

13. True or False: Small, incremental measurements can be the most economical measurement strategy.

True

False

14. You need _____ data to significantly reduce uncertainty in cases where uncertainty is already _____.

A. More, high

B. More, low

C. Less, high

D. Less, low

E. B and C

F. A and D

15. Which of the following is the rough but simple approximation for estimating EVPI for one variable out of a decision with many uncertain variables?

A. Hold all variables at their mean, find the difference between the highest and lowest figures, and compute an information value for the difference. Multiply this value by the number of variables.

B. Choose a random variable and subtract its value from the mean of all the figures; then square the difference. Do this with each variable.

C. For each variable, find the threshold where the decision is a breakeven while holding all other variables at their mean. Compute its information value with that threshold, return its value to its mean, and repeat with the next variable.

D. Find the threshold for each value and rank order the values from highest to lowest. Take the second and second from last figures and compute their EVIs. For each figure, use the average of it and either the second or second from last values, depending on which it is closer to in rank order.

16. What patterns did the author notice in his analysis of IT investments prior to 1999 and later in the analysis of other types of decisions?

A. There was evidence for the measurement inversion.

B. The majority of variables in decision models had high information values.

   C. The most time was being spent on high information value
      measurements.
   D. All of the above
   E. A and C

17. Which of the following is an example of measurement inversion?
    A. An accountant using QuickBooks to determine employee earnings
    B. A manager measuring time spent on projects while ignoring their
       long-term benefits
    C. Measuring the adoption rate of new technology
    D. Measuring the effects of sales training on sales rather than sales
       training attendance

18. Up to this point in the book, we have learned how to do which of
    the following?
    A. Determine current uncertainty
    B. Compute the value of a measurement
    C. Design a way of conducting a measurement
    D. All of the above
    E. A and B

19. Typical IQ tests are often based on normally distributed sample
    scores with a mean of 100 and a standard deviation of 15. What
    is the percentage chance of a random individual receiving a score
    under 85?

20. Suppose you are trying to determine whether to fund a new busi-
    ness venture. You estimate that the probability of failure would be
    20% and the cost of failure would be $100,000. You consider this
    risk acceptable and decide that, without further measurements, your
    default decision is to accept the investment. Calculate the Expected
    Opportunity Loss (EOL).

21. Assume you are trying to predict the number of units of a product that will be sold. Compute a Relative Threshold (RT) using the following information and the chart provided in the book.
    - Threshold = 6,000 units
    - Worst bound (WB) = 4,000 units
    - Best bound (BB) = 10,000 units

22. Using the RT you've just calculated, compute the EVPI, assuming an opportunity loss per unit of $50.

23. A warehouse manager decides to stock a product at an amount twice as high as expected demand. Describe a condition where this is rational.

24. Draw and label the components of an EVI/ECI/EVPI chart.

25. **Challenge:** Using discrete approximation methods, construct a spreadsheet to compute the information value for the demand on some product using a bidirectional and symmetrical loss function.

    You are the owner of a retail store and you need to commit to an order of a product in advance of the upcoming holiday shopping season. If the product is overstocked or understocked by one unit, there is a loss of inventory costs or a loss of sales, respectively. Assume both of these losses are the same. Your spreadsheet should be able to take any 90% CI for demand and any unit loss rate and compute the total EVPI. Since the loss function is symmetrical, simply assume your estimate is the center of whatever range you enter. For example, if the 90% CI is 1,000 to 2,000 units, take the best estimate to be 1,500. Assume then an overstocking/understocking loss for each unit over/under this midpoint.

CHAPTER 8

The Transition: From What to Measure to How to Measure

LEARNING OBJECTIVES

- Define "measurement instrument" and describe seven advantages of its use.
- Use "decomposition" to further reduce uncertainty of a variable.
- Review the tips provided for conducting secondary research.
- Describe some basic methods of observation for the proposed object of measurement.
- Outline the considerations for a measurement expenditure relative to EVPI.
- Describe the differences between systemic and random error, describe the differences between measurement accuracy and precision, and discuss the benefits of random sampling.
- Outline and give an example of three types of observation bias.

CHAPTER OVERVIEW

Chapter 8 gives us strategies to determine what type of measurement methods to use and discusses the concept of measurement instruments. The benefits to decomposition are outlined, including that they may make further measurements unnecessary. Benefits of conducting secondary research and a variety of empirical methods for describing the object of measurement are given. The Expected Value of Perfect Information (EVPI) should be a guideline for measurement effort.

All measurements have error, and different types of error as well as measurement accuracy and precision are important to consider. Types of bias are outlined. The chapter closes by summarizing methods for identifying a measurement instrument and offering general tips for their use.

QUESTIONS

1. Which of the following questions need(s) to be asked in order to determine which category of measurement methods to use?
    A. What are the parts of the thing we're uncertain about?
    B. What are the sources of error?
    C. How do the "observables" identified lend themselves to measurement?
    D. All of the above
    E. B and C

2. Which of the following are examples of measurement instruments?
    A. Thermometer
    B. Geiger counter
    C. Question on a test
    D. All of the above
    E. A and B

3. True or False: Measurement instruments that don't eliminate uncertainty are useless.
    True
    False

4. Which of the following is *not* a characteristic of an instrument?
    A. They detect what you can't.
    B. They are all complex and should be used only by specialists.
    C. They can be calibrated to account for some error.
    D. They can aid reasoning and memory by doing quick calculations and storing the result.

5. True or False: The following is an example of a measurement instrument: Around 4000 B.C., inhabitants of the Zagros region of Iran used clay tokens to represent numbers of sheep.
   True
   False

6. Which of the following is an example of a decomposition?
   A. Counting the number of marbles in a jar
   B. Estimating the cost of a construction project by estimating the cost of several components of the project, then totaling them
   C. Observing and recording the number of people at a fair
   D. Using a galvanometer to detect electric current

7. True or False: Decomposition can sometimes make further measurements unnecessary.
   True
   False

8. Name some search terms that are more likely to produce quantitative results if you are searching the impact of sales training on sales.

9. Suppose you have identified an uncertainty that doesn't seem to leave a trail of any kind. Which question(s) could you ask next?
   A. If the trail doesn't already exist, can you observe it directly or at least a sample of it?
   B. If it doesn't appear to leave behind a detectable trail of any kind, and direct observation does not seem feasible without some additional aid, can you devise a way to begin to track it now?
   C. If tracking the existing conditions does not suffice (with either existing or newly collected data), can the phenomenon be "forced" to occur under conditions that allow easier observation?
   D. All of the above
   E. B and C

10. True or False: The method(s) from question 9 don't apply to forecasts.

    True

    False

11. Measurement precision is defined as low _____ error, regardless of the amount of _____ error.

    A. Random, systemic

    B. Systemic, random

    C. Biased, computational

    D. Temporary, persistent

12. Measurement accuracy is defined as low _____ error.

    A. Random

    B. Systematic

    C. Computational

    D. Persistent

13. True or False: In some fields, "reliable" is used to mean roughly the same thing as "precise," and "valid" is used to mean roughly the same thing as "accurate."

    True

    False

14. True or False: A thermometer that always produces a temperature that is 20 degrees higher than the actual temperature is precise but inaccurate.

    True

    False

15. You decide to try flipping a standard penny 1,001 times. Which of the following outcomes is more likely?

    A. Your first flip will come up "heads."

    B. Your next thousand flips will result in 500 +/– 26 heads.

16. You have just conducted an Internet-only survey on political party affiliation, and have assumed that you've reached a representative sample of the population. This is an example of which of the following biases?

    A. Expectancy bias
    B. Selection bias
    C. Observer bias

17. Suppose you wanted to estimate unproductive time spent by employees at a supermarket. How might you decompose this variable?

18. Write out at least three of the five tips for identifying a measurement instrument.

19. Explain what "empirical" means.

20. List two or more "Useful Measurement Assumptions."

21. Briefly explain why the author aims to spend about 2% to 10% of the Expected Value of Information (EVI) for initial measurement expenditures.

22. In the Kinsey sex study, what did Alfred Kinsey inaccurately presume about large nonrandom samples?

CHAPTER 9

Sampling Reality: How Observing Some Things Tells Us about All Things

---

LEARNING OBJECTIVES

- Learn how to compute 90% confidence intervals for the estimate of a mean, median, or population proportion based on a sample.
- Describe the impact of small samples in situations with high uncertainty.
- Describe variations on population proportion sampling.
- Describe the method for supporting a measurement relative to a threshold.
- Compute the probability that an experimental result is due to chance.
- Use regression modeling methods with Excel.
- Describe the meaning and limitations of significance testing.

CHAPTER OVERVIEW

Chapter 9 discusses some simple methods for making useful inferences from samples of a larger population. Examples are provided to help you develop an intuition for the concepts. The chapter shows that uncertainty reduction can be achieved with surprisingly few observations. Parametric and nonparametric statistics are distinguished, and "mathless" ways for computing 90% confidence intervals are presented.

Calculations for estimating the mean and median of a population are introduced, as well as variations on population proportion sampling. Methods for reducing uncertainty relative to some threshold, serial sampling, and controlled experiments are presented. The proper interpretation and limitations of significance testing are introduced. Finally, regression analysis methods are discussed.

QUESTIONS

1. Suppose you want to determine what percentage of businesses in Illinois use e-commerce. To do so, you survey 50 businesses to get a sense of the reality across the whole state. This is an example of taking a _____ of a _____.
   A. Population; sample
   B. Sample; population
   C. Sample; census
   D. Census; population

2. True or False: Suppose I have a sack of marbles and I ask you to give a 90% confidence interval for the average weight of one marble in grams. You guess between 20 and 180 grams. The weights of five randomly selected marbles are revealed to be 70, 73, 75, 71, and 80 grams. In light of this new information, you should probably widen your confidence interval.
   True
   False

3. True or False: William Sealy Gosset developed the Student's t-statistic to produce estimates based on samples smaller than what is recommended for estimates of population means using normal distribution.
   True
   False

4. Which of the following is/are true?
   A. When uncertainty is high, a few samples can greatly reduce uncertainty.

    B. Calibrated estimators cannot reduce uncertainty with a single sample.

    C. More math always reduces uncertainty for calibrated estimators.

    D. All of the above

    E. A and C

5. Which of the following is/are true?

    A. If 30 samples have already been taken, one needs to quadruple the sample size to get an expected reduction of roughly 50% of the width of the current 90% confidence interval.

    B. Sampling from infinite populations is not practical.

    C. When taking 20 samples, the last 10 samples probably reduced uncertainty more than the first 10 samples.

    D. B and C

    E. All of the above

6. True or False: If you know almost nothing about a population, you should never try to draw inferences from just a few samples.

    True

    False

7. Which of the following is/are true?

    A. From a highly homogeneous population (e.g., water in a large tank), very few samples or even one may suffice to reduce uncertainty.

    B. Estimates of a population mean will always converge if enough samples are taken.

    C. A normally distributed population will not produce a converging mean if the sample size is increased.

    D. Populations that follow a "power law" distribution might never produce a converging estimate of a mean regardless of sample size.

    E. A and D

8. Which of the following is/are true?

    A. Small samples can produce statistically significant results.

    B. Statistical significance refers to a minimum required sample size.

C. Statistical significance refers to whether the state of uncertainty was reduced.

D. Statistical significance refers to whether the measurement was economically justified.

E. A and D

9. If you have a sample size of 26, which two samples can you use to approximate the 90% confidence interval bounds for the median?
   A. The first and last
   B. The ninth largest and the ninth smallest
   C. The second largest and the second smallest
   D. The fourth largest and the fourth smallest

10. True or False: When using the "mathless" 90% confidence interval for the median, you don't have to make assumptions about the underlying population distribution.
    True
    False

11. Suppose you are trying to determine what percentage of the time actuaries at your insurance company use statistical software. You randomly poll 20 people at randomly selected times and ask what they are doing at the moment you poll them. Of those, four say they are using the statistical software at that moment. What kind of sample is this, and what is the 90% confidence interval for the share of time staff spend using this software?
    A. Spot, 9.9% to 38%
    B. Serial, 16.3% to 28%
    C. Student's t, 17% to 54%
    D. Stratified, 3% to 71%

12. What is the name of the sampling method that uses different methods and/or sample sizes for different groups within a sample?
    A. Spot
    B. Clustered

C. Stratified
D. Serial

13. A child's toy with small, removable parts is released to the public and then determined by the manufacturer to be a choking hazard. Investigators want to know how many of these hazardous toys are potentially being used by consumers. The company realizes a PR nightmare will ensue and decides to dissolve, resulting in the loss of reliable manufacturing and sales information that could link a part to a manufacturing date and site. It is known, however, that serial numbers are incremental with a step value of 1 (though it is not known which serial number is considered the lowest). Investigators later obtain a random sample of five toys with the following serial numbers:

   - 10099632, 10098502, 10107348, 10096364, and 10085197

   Determine a 90% confidence interval for the total number of toys produced.
   A. 17,529–70,138
   B. 29,004–75,852
   C. 13,749–18,582
   D. 23,812–66,453

14. Suppose you work for a city's sanitation department, and you'd like to determine the percentage of houses in the city that recycle. You select 100 blocks in the city, and ask every household on each of the 100 blocks. Which sampling method is this?
   A. Spot
   B. Clustered
   C. Stratified
   D. Mathless
   E. Normal

15. A drug company wants to test the effectiveness of two drugs (Drug A and Drug B) in curing headaches. The drug company has a total of three groups of people. The first group (Group 1) receives Drug A, the second group (Group 2) receives Drug B, and the third group

(Group 3) receives a sugar pill (placebo). Which of the three groups is considered the control group?

A. Group 1

B. Group 2

C. Group 3

D. None of the above

E. A and B

16. Suppose you're trying to determine whether a measure of personality extroversion is related to employee sales records. You administer a test to a random sample of 110 employees, and label the top 40 scorers as "extroverts." Here are the relative sales records:

   • 40 extroverts—mean of $35,000 in revenue, a sample standard deviation of 3,000

   • 70 control—mean of $34,000 in revenue, a sample standard deviation of 3,041.38

   Based on your sample information, determine the probability that the mean revenue of the population of extroverts is lower than the mean revenue of the rest of the population.

   A. 4.7%

   B. 11.2%

   C. 89.0%

   D. 97.9%

17. In an experiment that seeks to determine the effectiveness of new employee training at MegaCorp, a test group of new employees receives the new training, and the remaining new employees receive standard training and serve as the control group. All employees must take an exam at the end of the training. If statistical methods show a significant increase in exam scores for the test group of new employees, then the experimenters will conclude that the new training is more effective than the standard training. The _____ is that the new training is not better than the standard training.

   A. Null hypothesis

   B. Alternative hypothesis

   C. Significance level

   D. Confidence interval

18. A p-value represents which of the following?
    A. The chance that the results are a random fluke, given the observations.
    B. The chance of seeing the observed result or something more extreme, given that the results were a random fluke.
    C. The chance that the tested theory is true, given the observations.
    D. The chance of seeing the observed result, given that the tested claim is true.

19. Which of the following is the strongest correlation between two variables?
    A. −0.98
    B. 0
    C. 0.90
    D. −0.5

20. Which of the following is true?
    A. If two variables are correlated, it is always the case that one has caused the other.
    B. If two variables are correlated, this is not evidence that one has caused the other.
    C. Neither of the above is true.

21. True or False: With hypothesis testing, whether or not a result is significant can change depending on an arbitrarily set level of significance.
    True
    False

22. Using the five sample weights from question number 2 and the Student's *t*-test, compute a 90% confidence interval for the average marble weight (note, for a sample of five, the *t*-score is 2.13).

23. Suppose you are an ornithologist trying to determine the number of wekas (a small, flightless bird) in a large, fenced-in nature reserve in New Zealand. You catch and tag a random sample of 200, and

release them back into the reserve. After allowing for the birds to disperse, you again catch a random sample of 200, 34 of which were previously tagged. Provide a 90% confidence interval for the number of wekas in the New Zealand reserve.

24. Suppose you're trying to determine what percentage of employees at a large corporation take public transportation to get to work. From a random sample of 20, 9 say they do. Give a 90% confidence interval for the proportion of all employees who take public transportation to work. Use one of the power tools.

25. One method for scientific experimentation is to compare two groups, one that is held steady, meaning that their conditions are not changed in any particular way, while a special condition is applied to the other group. What is this method known as, and what are each of these two experimental groups called?

26. What is the correlation between the following series of numbers?
X: {1, 2, 3, 4, 5, 6, 7, 8, 9, 10}
Y: {11, 12, 13, 14, 15, 16, 17, 18, 19, 20}
You may use the appropriate Excel function.

27. Suppose you own a telemarketing company and you're trying to predict the number of clients acquired per month from the number of sales calls. You have the following figures from 12 individuals:

- Number of sales calls: 300, 418, 320, 601, 247, 381, 298, 376, 403, 328, 460, 411
- Clients acquired: 31, 18, 26, 45, 18, 29, 34, 40, 41, 17, 49, 30

What is the correlation between these two data sets? You may use the appropriate Excel function.

28. Using information from the last question, estimate the slope and intercept. You may use the appropriate Excel functions.

CHAPTER 10

Bayes: Adding to What You Know Now

LEARNING OBJECTIVES

- Describe what is meant by the "prior knowledge paradox."
- Apply the rules of conditional probability, including Bayes' theorem, to a simple business problem.
- Define the instinctive Bayesian approach and provide an example calculation and estimate.
- Define heterogeneous benchmarking and give an example application.
- Describe how prior knowledge in samples can be used to make inferences about a population.
- Describe how Bayes' theorem contradicts commonly held misconceptions about statistical inferences.

CHAPTER OVERVIEW

Chapter 10 provides an overview of Bayesian statistics. The method's utility for calibrated estimators is discussed, and example calculations are provided. Each of us has a "natural Bayesian instinct" that allows us to update calibrated estimates subjectively. The extent to which we are able to apply Bayesian methods to our calculations accurately is examined with an overview of research on the matter. By using what the author calls a "Bayesian correction," calibrated estimates can be made internally consistent.

Heterogeneous benchmarking, which is a means of updating prior knowledge based on somewhat dissimilar examples, is a helpful way of estimating highly uncertain quantities. Bayesian inversion is a method for adjusting an original calibrated estimate based on additional information. An example of such a calculation is described in detail. Measurements on a continuum for population proportion and estimate of a population mean are also described and calculated. The author discusses the application of Bayes' theorem to a matrix of interdependent observations and supplies a clear refutation of a measurement skeptic's fallacy.

QUESTIONS

1. According to the author, which of the following do introductory statistics textbooks overstate?
   A. Reliance on prior knowledge about a population
   B. The advantages of Bayesian over frequentist methods
   C. That the only thing you can know about a population is what you infer from your samples
   D. All of the above
   E. B and C

2. True or False: Bayesian statistics begin with knowledge you already have before you begin deliberate sampling.
   True
   False

3. True or False: Calibrated estimators should not be used for assigning prior probabilities.
   True
   False

4. True or False: Qualitative information is inadequate for updating prior probabilities.
   True
   False

5. A typical uncalibrated estimator _____.
   A. Is overconfident, tends to ignore prior knowledge, and emphasizes new data
   B. Ignores new data and emphasizes prior knowledge
   C. Balances overconfidence and underconfidence
   D. Is underconfident and overemphasizes prior knowledge and new data

6. True or False: Without use of priors, hypothesis testing can make conclusions about the probability that data more extreme than that observed in an experiment would have been observed, given that the null hypothesis is true.
   True
   False

7. Which of the following is an example of a heterogeneous benchmark?
   A. Using a random number within a certain range to estimate a quantity
   B. Using measurements of losses due to a system outage or lawsuit to estimate the losses due to a data breach.
   C. The "softer costs" likelihood of catastrophic events
   D. Using a 90% confidence interval to estimate gross margins on a financial report

8. True or False: Peter Tippett points out that the problem with the "wouldn't it be horrible if . . . " attitude in cyber security is that it doesn't allow for thoughtful prioritization of measurement problems.
   True
   False

9. A calibrated Bayesian estimator provides a range estimate for the average cost of purchases per visit at a fast-food restaurant of $20 to $30. Twelve subsequent random samples have produced a 90% confidence interval of $25 to $37 with a mean of $31. Which of the following is true?
   A. The mean of the updated range should be between $0 and $25.
   B. The mean of the updated range should be between $25 and $31.

C. The expert should abandon his original range and use only the sample data.

D. The expert should stick to his original range.

10. True or False: Bayes' theorem allows us to begin our measurement problems with this question, which is often easier to answer: "What is the probability of this observation if X were true?"

True

False

11. Given an initial prior probability or 90% confidence interval and subsequent sampling data, a new 90% confidence interval based on a Bayesian calculation should be which of the following?

A. Narrower than either one alone

B. The average of the width of the two

C. The same width as the prior probability

D. The same width as the sampling data

12. What step(s) is/are required to estimate the mean of a population using Bayesian methods?

A. A discrete number of potential population distributions needs to be identified and a prior probability needs to be assigned to each.

B. Each population distribution needs to be broken into discrete increments and the probability of each discrete increment needs to be estimated.

C. Student's t-statistic needs to be used to estimate each probability distribution.

D. A and B

E. B and C

13. Which of the following statements is true?

A. Bayesian methods cannot be applied to regression modeling.

B. Bayesian methods cannot be applied to controlled experiments.

C. The first sample can update probabilities in any application of Bayesian methods.

D. Higher-resolution methods require making thousands of individually assessed, separate calibrated estimates for all increments of all distributions.

14. Suppose you're estimating the probability of the purchase of your company's services by a prospect, which is considering a merger with another firm. Overall, an 85% chance that the purchase will occur is estimated [P(P) = 85%]. Based on experience, a calibrated estimator assigns a probability of 70% that the merger will go through [P(M) = 70%]. If the merger does go through, the estimator assigns a 50% chance that the prospect will purchase your company's services [P(P|M) = 50%]. If the merger doesn't go through, the estimator assigns a probability of 80% that the purchase will go through. Are these probabilities internally consistent? Why or why not?

15. One determinant of whether or not someone will be a good fighter pilot is whether or not they played with toy planes as a child. Given that a new fighter pilot graduates in the top half of his training class [P(H) = 50%], there's a 95% chance that he played with toy planes as a child [P(TP|H) = 95%]. Of the entire population of fighter pilots, about 75% of them played with toy planes as children [P(TP) = 75%]. Given that a fighter pilot played with toy planes as a child, what's the chance he would graduate in the top half of his class [P(H|TP)]?

16. For this question, consider that political party affiliation (Democrat or Republican) is related to living in either an urban or a rural setting, respectively. Using conditional probability notation, express the probability that a person is a Democrat, given that he or she lives in an urban setting, and show how it would be calculated using the probability that someone is a Democrat, the probability the person lives in an urban setting, and the conditional probability that the person lives in an urban setting given that he or she is a Democrat.

17. A man is suspicious that his spouse is cheating on him, and assigns an 80% probability that his suspicion is true. The man hires a private investigator because he thinks it's possible that the PI could find confirmatory evidence. After a two-week investigation, the PI finds no evidence of this. Does this constitute evidence that the spouse is *not* cheating on him? Why or why not?

18. Consider the following series of estimations:
- There's a 50% chance that a corporate acquisition will occur in one year.
- There's an 80% chance a company will have lower revenue after a year, assuming the acquisition occurs.
- There's a 60% chance a company will have lower revenue after a year, assuming the acquisition doesn't occur.

Add up the conditional probabilities to determine the probability that your revenue will be lower after a year.

19. List two or more controls you can use in the instinctive Bayesian approach to avoid errors in human judgment.

20. If you roll a fair six-sided die 20 times, what is the chance of getting exactly five 3s? Show the Excel function for computing this.

21. Suppose you're trying to decide whether to open a new retail store in a suburban town. Based on information from other stores in similar areas, a calibrated estimator produces a 90% confidence interval of 30% to 75% for the percentage of citizens who would shop there at least once a month. Based on this information, what is the chance that between 65% and 70% of the population proportion would end up shopping there? Include the Excel function.

22. Using information from question 21, suppose you conduct a survey in the town that asks individuals if they would visit the proposed store at least once a month. Out of 25 random individuals sampled, 17 said they would. Using Bayesian inversion, update your 90% confidence interval using the new information (you can use the spreadsheet on www.howtomeasureanything.com).

23. Consider the following facts about the detection of a certain disease in human patients:
    - The test produces a positive result 95% of the time when the person has the disease.
    - The test produces a positive result 0.5% of the time when the patient does not have the disease.
    - The overall prevalence of the disease in the population is one in 100,000 people.

    Compute the probability a person has the disease given a positive test result, and show your work.

24. In Emily Rosa's experiment, what variable would represent the prior probability?

Preference and Attitudes: The Softer Side of Measurement

LEARNING OBJECTIVES

- Describe why "value" measurements are necessarily subjective and the difference between stated and revealed preferences.
- Describe four major categories of survey questions as well as five tips for avoiding response bias.
- Explain how "willingness to pay" and "Value of a Statistical Life" can be used for measuring value.
- Explain what is problematic about moral arguments against the quantitative valuation of life.
- Describe how investment boundaries can be used to quantify risk tolerance.
- Describe how utility curves can be used for quantifying subjective trade-offs.
- Explain the advantages of profit maximization versus purely subjective trade-offs.

CHAPTER OVERVIEW

Chapter 11 emphasizes the measurements related to subjective preferences and attitudes. Stated and revealed preferences are described, and why revealed preferences might be better indicators is discussed. There are a variety of techniques, including surveys, that are used to measure these phenomena, and guidelines for their appropriate usage are provided.

It is helpful to consider valuation problems in the context of trade-offs, and the author provides a consulting example about the value of community support. Controversial measurement challenges like the quantitative valuation of life are also examined.

Investment boundaries are a helpful way to quantify your risk tolerance as a function of expected return on investment (ROI) and the chance of negative ROI. This is a special case of utility curves, which can be used to unambiguously quantify preferences for trade-offs between multiple competing objectives. While many trade-offs preferences can only be described subjectively, the author points out examples where trade-offs that initially seem purely subjective are actually forecasts about objective observable outcomes.

QUESTIONS

1. True or False: In a way, all measurements about economic value are subjective because they depend on human preferences.
   True
   False

2. If you wanted survey respondents to quantify with an ordinal response their level of agreement with a statement (e.g., "I am satisfied with this product"), which type of response option would work best?
   A. Likert scale
   B. Multiple choice
   C. Rank order
   D. Open ended

3. If you wanted survey respondents to describe their detailed opinions with minimal influence by the structure of the questionnaire, which type of response option would work best?
   A. Likert scale
   B. Multiple choice
   C. Rank order
   D. Open ended

4. True or False: You can correlate subjective responses to objective measures.

   True

   False

5. Willingness to pay (WTP) surveys have been used to value the avoidance of loss in which of the following scenarios?

   A. Avoiding the loss of an endangered species

   B. Improving public health

   C. Improvements to the environment

   D. All of the above

   E. B and C

6. Which of these is NOT a strategy to reduce response bias mentioned in the book?

   A. Avoid compound questions.

   B. Avoid leading questions.

   C. Avoid open-ended questions.

   D. Avoid loaded terms.

7. Which of these statements is true about Modern Portfolio Theory (MPT)?

   A. It was first developed by Harry Markowitz in the 1950s.

   B. The theory has become the basis for most portfolio optimization methods.

   C. The theory tries to quantify how risk analysis affects portfolios using Monte Carlo simulations.

   D. All of the above

   E. A and B

8. Which response-bias reduction rule does the following question violate?: "Should the government raise taxes further and spend more on education or defense?"

   A. Keep the question precise and short.
   B. Avoid loaded terms.
   C. Avoid leading questions.
   D. Avoid compound questions.
   E. Reverse questions to avoid response set bias.

9. Which response-bias reduction rule does the following question violate?: "Brand X was recently named the highest-quality brand in the world. How satisfied are you with your Brand X product?"

   A. Keep the question precise and short.
   B. Avoid loaded terms.
   C. Avoid leading questions.
   D. Avoid compound questions.
   E. Reverse questions to avoid response set bias.

10. Suppose you're trying to avoid response set bias by reversing questions. You determine that too many would be scored the same way if the participant agreed with the statements. Which would be an appropriate adjustment for the following statement?: "I often make online payments with a credit card."

    A. I don't often make online payments with a credit card.
    B. I often make online payments with electronic checks.
    C. I don't often make online payments with electronic checks.
    D. I never make online payments.

11. True or False: In general, more can be learned from stated preferences than from revealed preferences.
    True
    False

12. What type of curve might a manager use to quantify preferences for productivity and error rates of employees? Example: An employee with a productivity rate of 100% and an error-free rate of 93% is equivalent to an employee with a productivity rate of 96% and an error-free rate of 96%.

    A. Quality curve
    B. Utility curve
    C. Productivity curve
    D. Trade-off curve

13. Which of these statements is/are characteristics of the certain monetary equivalent (CME)?

    A. A CME can help prioritize investments when there are a variety of risks and different ways of looking at returns.
    B. The CME of an investment is the fixed and certain dollar amount that the investor considers just as good as the uncertain set of possible returns.
    C. A CME can only be estimated for the valuation of certain outcomes.
    D. All of the above
    E. A and B

14. Consider a survey of network administrators assessing the average duration of network outages under various conditions. You are considering the following versions of responses for that survey question—we'll call them response sets X and Y. According to Craig Fox's research, in which of the following response sets would a respondent be more likely to choose response option A?

    Response Set X:
    A. 0–14 minutes
    B. 15–30 minutes
    C. 31–45 minutes
    D. 46–60 minutes

    Response Set Y:
    A. 0–14 minutes
    B. 15–30 minutes
    C. 31–45 minutes
    D. 46–60 minutes
    E. 61–75 minutes
    F. 76–90 minutes

15. How did Andrew Oswald measure the value of happiness?

    A. He used a series of personality inventories and compared their results to publicly available demographic data.

    B. He asked people how happy they were, surveyed recent life events, asked them how much money they were making, and estimated their happiness as a function of their income and life events.

    C. He divided subjects into experimental and control conditions and subjected one to positive and one to negative life events, and compared these findings with income and other demographic information.

    D. He used the Value of a Statistical Life (VSL) formula to approximate subjective happiness in combination with a survey of relevant life events.

16. Which of the following is the basis for the calculation of VSL?

    A. How much people are willing to pay to reduce the chance of an early death by some small amount

    B. People respond to an open-ended question that asks them how much they value their own lives.

    C. Experts vote on how much individuals value their lives.

    D. None of the above

17. What did Dr. James Hammitt find confounds individuals' thinking about their preferences?

    A. Indecisiveness of opinion

    B. Overly flexible cognitive styles

    C. A level of mathematical illiteracy

    D. An underemphasis on the weighting of qualitative information

18. Though it has many useful components, the author has criticized which theoretical assumption of Modern Portfolio Theory?

    A. Market volatility modeled using a normal distribution

    B. Market volatility modeled using a uniform distribution

    C. The capital asset pricing model

    D. That all investors aim to maximize economic utility

19. What does a typical risk/return boundary chart (as shown in Exhibit 11.2) suggest about preferences of risk and return in investments?

A. As expected ROI increases, maximum acceptable risk increases.

B. People accept less risk as ROI increases.

C. There's a minimum level of risk people accept regardless of ROI.

D. At zero risk, people are willing to accept a zero return.

20. True or False: Two quantitatively savvy members of the same company, given the same information, would likely construct identical investment boundaries for their company (assume they work in separate rooms).

True

False

21. A 15% increase in the number of customers who say they're satisfied with the call is considered equal in value to a 10% decrease in call duration at the current satisfaction level. Which of the following would *necessarily* be considered preferable to either of these states?

A. A 14% increase in customer satisfaction or a 12% increase in call duration

B. A 7.5% increase in customer satisfaction and a 5% decrease in call duration

C. A 13% increase in customer satisfaction

D. A 16% increase in customer satisfaction and no increase in call duration

22. True or False: Multiple points on the same utility curve are considered equally valuable.

True

False

23. Consider a utility curve chart where the axes are on-time completion rate (OCR) and error-free rate (EFR) for software projects. More of both is desirable if possible. A 95% OCR and 95% EFR are on the same curve as a 90% OCR and 98% EFR. Which of the following statements is necessarily true?

A. An OCR of 90% and an EFR of 96% are preferable to a 95% OCR and 95% EFR.

B. A random point on the middle curve is equal in value to a random point on the bottom curve.

C. A 95% OCR will always be preferable to a 94% OCR even when EFR decreases.

D. An OCR of 95% and an EFR of 95% are preferable to an OCR of 90% and an EFR of 97%.

24. What is a potential problem with utility curves?

A. Factors can't be monetized.

B. Things that seem like subjective trade-offs may be factors for predicting objective outcomes.

C. They don't allow for subjective valuation.

D. All of the above

25. Why is it necessary to quantify and document the risk versus return preferences of an organization?

A. Irrelevant external factors affect the risk aversion of decision makers. Using the same documented and quantified preferences would remove this random variation.

B. Decision makers are systematically too risk tolerant.

C. It removes subjectivity from risk and return preferences.

D. All of the above

26. Where would a WTP survey be most relevant?

A. To determine how much productivity would have to increase to justify an investment in software

B. To determine how much air travelers might value shorter lines at security

C. To determine how much profit would be increased by purchasing newer manufacturing equipment

D. To estimate the risk of travel

27. True or False: Overall performance generally has too many subjective, qualitative components to be measured efficiently.
True
False

28. Explain why an individual who lives an ordinary lifestyle, partaking of typical creature comforts, can be considered hypocritical for calling human life "priceless."

29. Suppose you're trying to decide between two bonuses: $25,000 in cash or 7,000 shares of company stock. If you're truly indifferent between these two, what is the certain monetary equivalent (CME) of all 7,000 stock shares combined?

30. Why does Paul Strassman subtract the costs of purchases, taxes, cost of money, and a few other items when he computes return on management?

CHAPTER 12

The Ultimate Measurement Instrument: Human Judges

LEARNING OBJECTIVES

- Describe and give an example of the anchoring bias, the halo/horns effect, the bandwagon bias, and emerging preferences.
- Describe how research by Meehl, Dawes, and others has undermined the assumed authority of experts.
- Explain the benefit of Rasch Models, and create and calculate a scenario in which they would be helpful.
- Explain the benefit of Lens Models, and create and calculate a scenario in which they would be helpful.
- Explain several problems with subjective weighted arbitrary scoring methods.
- Describe the relative efficiency of the various types of models described in the chapter.

CHAPTER OVERVIEW

Chapter 12 begins with an overview of the advantages and disadvantages of the human mind as a measurement instrument. Despite our strengths, we are prone to a variety of biases, including anchoring, the halo/horns effect, bandwagon bias, and emerging preferences. There is a large, consistent body of research demonstrating the inferiority of unaided human intuition relative to quantitative models across a range of domains. However, human experts can still be used as a type of measurement instrument, especially after controlling for some known types of errors.

The Rasch Model provides a simple way to adjust probabilities in situations like differing standards among judges in their ratings. Similar improvements can be achieved with Lens Models, which use hypothetical scenarios that are rated by experts, then combined through regression models. Unfortunately, businesses tend not to use these types of empirical strategies and instead use methods such as ordinal scales, which are problematic for a variety of reasons. Objective historical models tend to be the most accurate, though historical data is sometimes unavailable.

QUESTIONS

1. Which of the following are examples of advantages of the human mind over typical measurement instruments?
   A. Making inferences in complex situations with large numbers of variables
   B. Consistency
   C. Summarizing large amounts of data
   D. Ability to assess ambiguous situations

2. In a 1974 study by Tversky and Kahneman, participants were given five seconds to give an intuitive estimation of the product of the numbers one to eight. The first group is presented with "$1 \times 2 \times 3 \times 4 \times 5 \times 6 \times 7 \times 8$" and the second is shown the numbers in reverse order. The second group gives much higher answers as a whole (2,250 vs. 512). Which bias does this demonstrate?
   A. Anchoring
   B. Halo/horns effect
   C. Bandwagon bias
   D. Emerging preferences

3. Three different groups were asked to estimate how far a dot of light moved in a pitch-black room (it did not actually move, but appeared to). Estimates were given out loud, and group responses differed dramatically due to social pressure. Which bias does this demonstrate?
   A. Anchoring
   B. Halo/horns effect
   C. Bandwagon bias
   D. Emerging preferences

4. True or False: When calculating the accuracy of expert predictions of movie box office sales, the author found a correlation of greater than 0.3.
   True
   False

5. In a nutshell, what was Paul Meehl's major conclusion in *Clinical versus Statistical Prediction*?
   A. Clinical judgment yields accuracy that is superior to quantitative models.
   B. Experts tend to be less accurate in their predictions than quantitative models.
   C. Experts are incapable of making predictions.
   D. Experts are better at predictions in business than in clinical psychology.

6. Which of the following is one of the most common reasons for the judgmental limitations of experts?
   A. Overconfidence
   B. Underconfidence
   C. Tendency to draw conclusions too slowly and carefully
   D. Attempts to quantify large amounts of information

7. What was the advantage of Dr. Ram's basic innovation for faculty evaluation?
   A. He implemented a more sophisticated regression-based algorithm.
   B. He recruited more individuals to participate in the review process.
   C. He organized the data in a way that could be more reliably interpreted.
   D. He used Rasch Models to mitigate the influence of varying standards among judges.

8. True or False: A major reason for the success of the simplest unweighted linear models is that individuals tend to begin with methods that are even more error-prone.
   True
   False

9. Which of the following is claimed by the basic principle of invariant comparison?
   A. Different measurement instruments should always give the same score.
   B. Different measurement instruments must always give different scores.
   C. Different measurement instruments should reliably tell you when one object of measurement is more than another.
   D. Different measurement instruments should reliably tell you when one variable is more precise than another.

10. Which of the following are problems that Rasch Models can adjust for?
    A. Different judges with different evaluation standards
    B. A single judge's tendency to give unreliable ratings due to his or her varying state of mind
    C. The overconfidence of experts in their predictions
    D. The difficulty that individuals have creating quantitative models

11. True or False: Egon Brunswik was more concerned with modeling internal thought processes than describing how decision parameters correlated with observed decision outcomes.
    True
    False

12. What is/are a general advantage(s) of using Lens Models to combine expert judgments?
    A. Lens Models are more consistent and reliable than experts.
    B. Lens Models allow us to combine more sets of judgments.
    C. Lens Models produce nonquantitative results that anyone can interpret.
    D. All of the above
    E. A and B

13. True or False: For business decisions, linear Lens Models will always produce the best possible accuracy.
    True
    False

14. What does the author's observations of business measurement solutions suggest about common business quantitative practices?
    A. What some businesses consider measurements are actually deterministic business cases that do not technically involve measurements.
    B. Businesses rarely or never use quantitative methods.
    C. Rasch Models are frequently used, but Lens Models are not.
    D. Decompositions are used less frequently than measurements.

15. With the use of ordinal scales, at times there is a false consensus on underlying risk that may add additional error. This is an example of which of the following?
    A. Partition dependence
    B. The illusion of communication
    C. Range compression

16. What are some key problems with the alternative "Information Economics" approach reviewed by the author?
    A. Definitions and weights are not tied to scientific approaches.
    B. The method undermines valid ROI calculations.
    C. The name is a misnomer.
    D. There are problems associated with ordinal scales like range compression and partition dependence
    E. All of the above

17. True or False: Usage of eigenvalues is evidence that Analytic Hierarchy Process (AHP) is theoretically and empirically sound.
    True
    False

18. For business cases, what is an advantage of Lens and Rasch Models over historical models?
    A. Historical models are less accurate.
    B. Documented historical data often isn't available whereas experts are available.
    C. Lens and Rasch Models are substantially easier to construct.
    D. Lens and Rasch Models require less expert judgment.

19. Which of the following statements about the relative efficacy of different human judgment models is correct?

  A. Lens and Rasch Models probably represent an improvement over simple linear models with standardized z-scores.

  B. Objective models work better without historical data.

  C. AHP has the most evidence of improving expert judgment.

  D. Ordinal scales may not be effective, but at least it is not possible for ordinal scales to have more error than unaided human judgment.

20. Compute the log-odds for an item that has a 40% probability using an Excel function.

21. What does a log-odds of zero convert to for a probability?

CHAPTER 13

New Measurement Instruments for Management

LEARNING OBJECTIVES

- Discuss the potential for new technologies as measurement tools.
- Give several examples of Internet sources that have been used as measurement tools.
- Give reasons for the accuracy of prediction markets and circumstances in which they are most useful.
- Describe how prediction markets work using an example about betting on predictions.

CHAPTER OVERVIEW

Chapter 13 discusses some of the more cutting-edge measurement instruments and the vast amount of potential they possess for measurement problems. GPS and the rise of various self-tracking technologies yield valuable insights. The Internet itself is an instrument, and the measurement insights it's capable of generating are vast. Screen-scrapers and application program interfaces provide continuously updated information about data from websites, and there are enormous possible combinations of data sources.

A particularly powerful approach to using the Internet as a measurement tool comes in the form of prediction markets, which aggregate many opinions into usable predictive tools. The method is superior to perhaps any individual in a given market. Examples of relevant sites and share betting, as well as an overview of their accuracy relative to other methods, are provided. The chapter closes with an example of how a research agency missed out on a chance to use prediction markets due to several basic misconceptions about their use.

QUESTIONS

1. The Quantified Self is a movement to incorporate technology into acquiring data that can be used for what purposes?

   A. Measuring health trends

   B. Tracking activity levels

   C. Detecting disease

   D. All of the above

   E. B and C

2. What did Freeman Dyson identify as the most revolutionary new measurement instrument?

   A. RFID

   B. Screen-scrapers

   C. GPS

   D. Light sheet microscope

3. True or False: Dr. Eysenbach was able to match but not beat traditional hospital reporting methods for flu outbreak predictions.

   True

   False

4. True or False: What is searched on Google, said on Twitter, and bought on eBay can all be publicly accessed.

   True

   False

5. According to the author, why are Internet screen-scrapers so convenient for researchers?

   A. They are typically available as freeware.

   B. Services like YouTube and Google Earth provide them as tools for direct access to their data.

   C. They can extract data about changes in Internet usage that occur frequently.

   D. They allow individuals to document personal quantitative health information.

6. What is a mash-up?

   A. A variety of tools that are independently useful for measurement problems

   B. A way to gather information from the Internet on a nearly constant basis from a single source

   C. Tools that use data from multiple sources presented in a way that provides new insight

   D. Power tools that combine regression and correlational techniques

7. What is an efficient stock market to an economist?

   A. One that is predictable

   B. One that is very hard to beat consistently

   C. One that has a high value

   D. One that is relatively easy to beat consistently

8. According to the author, why are prediction markets better for forecasting than opinion polls?

   A. Participants have an incentive to consider the questions carefully and expend their own resources for new information.

   B. Opinion polls can rarely reach more than 50 people.

   C. There is no evidence of "herd instinct" with prediction markets.

   D. Most people don't like to share their opinions.

9. Which of the following is a characteristic of an adaptive survey approach?
   A. It provides a standardized template for the implementation of many analysis techniques.
   B. It might present different questions to different respondents.
   C. It is a data collection technique that enhances the accuracy of catch-recatch methods.
   D. It is a survey technique that uses visual aids for collecting emotional response data.

10. Which of the following is true about the predictions made by markets that use "play money"?
    A. Real money exchanges are slightly less well calibrated.
    B. Prediction markets require fewer participants and are more difficult to update with new information than Lens Models.
    C. Prediction securities are consistently underpriced compared to their chance of coming true.
    D. Applying an adjustment factor could potentially yield predictions as accurate as other markets like Foresight Exchange or News Futures.

11. Which of the following is a good condition for using prediction markets to make subjective assessments?
    A. The subjective assessments are time-dependent.
    B. There's only one individual making assessments.
    C. Forecasting isn't required.
    D. Opinions are aggregated at only a single point in time.

12. True or False: If the price of a certain prediction market security increases, then the newest information that forecasters are considering about the probability of the event reflects that it is less likely than the aggregate opinion before the price increase.
    True
    False

13. Which of the following errors of judgment was/were made when DARPA was accused of "spending taxpayer dollars to create terrorism betting parlors"?

    A. The issue was framed as being about the morality of gambling as opposed to objective measures of performance.

    B. It was simply assumed that the program would not be effective.

    C. It was assumed that this method would displace other intelligence-gathering methods.

    D. All of the above

    E. B and C

14. What technologies does GPS Insight combine to provide flexible location data?

15. What has been problematic about past social science research methods on time spent with friends, and how have new technologies helped?

16. Describe the method Dr. Gunther Eysenbach use to anticipate flu outbreaks.

17. Identify three or more ways people can leave a digital footprint on the Internet.

18. Why do some web-based service providers discourage the use of screen-scrapers, and what alternatives do they provide to developers to discourage this?

19. Through their resourceful measurements, what was National Leisure Group able to conclude about their customers' experiences? What changes did they then make?

20. Identify at least two issues that have been successfully tracked or forecasted using social networks.

21. Identify at least two trends that have been successfully tracked or forecasted using Google Trends.

22. Briefly explain whether prediction markets work well for assessing probabilities.

CHAPTER 14

A Universal Measurement Method: Applied Information Economics

LEARNING OBJECTIVES

- Briefly describe the background to the author's development of Applied Information Economics.
- Learn the five-step framework and explain how it applies to each of the cases.
- Outline the four phases for each of the three cases.
- Describe some considerations for measuring quality, value, innovation, information availability, and flexibility.
- Describe how flexibility measurements relate to options theory.
- Briefly summarize the philosophy behind Applied Information Economics.

CHAPTER OVERVIEW

Chapter 14 combines the lessons of the book into a chapter outlining the steps and philosophy behind Applied Information Economics. The author reveals a bit about his background and the development of the method. The process can be broken up into four phases.

Three practical case examples are provided to elucidate Applied Information Economics. We are shown how to value a system that monitors your drinking water, forecast fuel for the Marine Corps, and measure the value of standards. A few final examples of measurements of quality, value, innovation, information availability, and flexibility are provided. The chapter closes with a summary of the Applied Information Economics philosophy.

QUESTIONS

1. What is the difference between the way the author and the attendees at the Chicago Club define whether an investment is "strategic"?
   A. AIE would never reject a "strategic" investment.
   B. The attendees at the Chicago Club wouldn't attempt to quantify risk.
   C. AIE doesn't attempt to compute ROI.
   D. All of the above
   E. A and C

2. What is the purpose of Phase 0 of the Applied Information Economics (AIE) process?

3. List the activities involved in Phase 1 of the Applied Information Economics process.

4. List the activities involved in Phase 2 of the Applied Information Economics process.

5. List the activities involved in Phase 3 of the Applied Information Economics process.

6. For the SDWIS case, it was ultimately necessary to reduce uncertainty about which of the following?
   A. Efficiency improvements
   B. State adoption rates of the technology
   C. The net economic benefits of drinking water policies
   D. Improved reporting rates

7. In the first phase of the Marine Corps case, the forecasting problem is clarified. Which specific forecasting problem was identified?
   A. Required fuel use, predicted 60 days in advance, for all ground forces of a single Marine Expeditionary Force
   B. Total fuel use of ground forces over the course of the conflict
   C. Total fuel use of aviation per week
   D. Total fuel use of trucks and Humvees per month

8. What did the Value of Information Analysis for the Marine Corps conclude about various individual information values?
   A. The likelihood of enemy contact was a significant predictor of fuel requirements.
   B. It was justified to continue to estimate a total fuel requirement, and then quadruple it in order to safely account for any margin of error.
   C. The details about convoy routes, including distances and surface conditions, warranted additional measurement efforts.
   D. It was critical to further measure tank fuel requirements, as this type of equipment is less fuel-efficient than other equipment (e.g., Humvees).

9. In each of the cases presented in Chapter 14, resources were allocated to additional measurement efforts to refine variable estimates when *and only when* which of the following?
   A. The variable was relatively easy to measure.
   B. The variable was considered by decision makers or other stakeholders, based on their intuition or previous experience, to be an important one.
   C. The calculated information value justified the measurement effort.
   D. The initial uncertainty was very high.

10. W. Edwards Deming defines quality roughly as the consistency with which expectations are met. Which of the following statements characterizes the author's views on this definition?
    A. It shouldn't depend on use of customer surveys.
    B. It is necessary for the concept of quality measurement, but not sufficient.

C. It is accurate and sufficient.

D. It is basically incoherent and shouldn't be taken seriously.

11. True or False: Questions of value necessarily imply alternatives.
    True
    False

12. True or False: For net present value (NPV) calculations, AIE takes into account the imperfection of information about future values.
    True
    False

13. True or False: Having a basic understanding of random sampling methods, how to set up and conduct controlled experiments, or how to improve expert judgment can significantly reduce uncertainty, but in order to implement any of these methods you must have a PhD in statistics.
    True
    False

14. True or False: The five-step framework of the Applied Information Economics (AIE) process ends with computing the value of additional information and measuring high-value uncertainties.
    True
    False

15. In the SDWIS case example, there was a list of nearly 100 variables at play in the model. Would additional efforts to further measure each, or even many, of the variables have been justified? Why or why not?

16. In the ACORD case, describe how the value of standards was decomposed and how it was measured.

17. Identify at least one decision an innovation measurement affects. Go into sufficient detail to identify a decision to use for a quantitative model.

18. Describe how you might decompose any idea(s) you provided for question 17. Ensure the decomposition is detailed enough for a quantitative calculation if values were provided for individual variables.

19. What might be measured with a bibliometric method and why?

20. What suggestions does the author have for decomposing information availability?

21. Suppose you're trying to determine whether to upgrade the equipment at your manufacturing firm, and you decide to measure flexibility. Flexibility is an ambiguous term that might easily be perceived as "immeasurable," but you know better. Discuss how you would decompose the idea of flexibility, both theoretically and with examples.

22. According to the author, options theory may be overemphasized as a measurement tool for flexibility. What assumption of Options Theory does the author challenge that is similar to an assumption made by Modern Portfolio Theory?

23. Summarize six points the author makes about the AIE philosophy.

PART II

Answers

CHAPTER 1

The Challenge of Intangibles

1. A
2. D
3. B
4. A
5. C
6. C
7. D
8. D
9. A
10. C
11. A
12. C
13. B
14. False
15. F
16. C
17. A
18. B
19. E
20. Misconceptions mentioned in this chapter include: that precise equations don't address messy real-world problems, and that using statistics requires advanced training.
21. Answers will vary but some good examples are public image, risk, quality, charisma, innovativeness, happiness, and complexity, and there are many more.
22. Define a decision problem.
23. When no further measurement variables have information values that would justify the cost of any additional measurement.

CHAPTER 2

An Intuitive Measurement Habit: Eratosthenes, Enrico, and Emily

1. A
2. B
3. C
4. D
5. False
6. E
7. D
8. True
9. F
10. C
11. False
12. The position of the sun over Syene, the angle of shadows cast by objects in Alexandria at the same time, and the distance between the two cities.
13. Answers may vary but should include some version of the following: "We can't even begin to guess at something like that," or "They dwell on the overwhelming uncertainties and/or the (presumed) prohibitive cost of making a measurement.
14. Ask a random sample of customers to determine if they could even tell the difference between pre-MII and post-MII deliverables. Whether improved quality had recently caused them to purchase more services from Mitre could also be an answer.

15. No, the market is already saturated according to the threshold set by the parent company. Average commissions per agency are \$129,424 per year, which is less than the required \$500,000.

16. Answers will vary. The student might consider the number of car owners, the frequency with which people visit car washes, the number of car wash businesses already operating in the area, etc.

17. Again, answers will vary, but might include consideration of the population of Dallas, how often a person visits a dentist on average, the number of patients a dentist might see in a day, and so on.

18. Earth's circumference is approximately 25,000 miles. Because the difference in angles the sun makes at noon is one-hundredth of an arc of a circle, the distance between cities is one-hundredth of the circumference of the earth. $250 \times 100 = 25,000$.

19. The approximate yield of the first atomic bomb using a handful of confetti.

20. The solution could include a method for comparing the judgments of different trained specialists. You make arrangements to ensure the specialists will be unaware that they are interviewing the same set of employees. You could ask each specialist to make a simple ranking of the employees—perhaps just indicating who is in the bottom half of employees and who is in the top half. Even if the specialists were guessing each time, there is a 50% chance that two specialists will agree on the ranking of an employee. If the specialists don't agree with each other any more than half the time, then they probably don't possess a useful leadership measurement tool. The harder way to do this might be to track employees over time or put them in different leadership positions and compare how they do based on performance or evaluations by subordinates and superiors. But this "hard" way is not necessary if the interviewers don't even agree. Other answers might include the use of remotely conducted interviews so that the interviewers aren't simply influenced by arbitrary factors like height and attractiveness.

CHAPTER 3

The Illusion of Intangibles:
Why Immeasurables Aren't

1. D
2. D
3. D
4. C
5. A
6. B
7. C
8. A
9. E
10. A
11. A
12. Answers will vary, but should discuss specific things that are observable and why they are relevant. Specifically, imagine two possible states of the item in question, such as one having more and another with less "customer satisfaction." Then imagine what is observed to be different in those situations.
13. Clarification chain
14. False
15. D
16. True
17. False
18. C

19. D

20. C

21. A

22. A

23. D

24. A patient might not have committed suicide.

25. Customer satisfaction matters, so it must be detectable. It can certainly be detected, so it must be detectable as an amount; for example, as the percentage of customers who return multiple times, which can be measured.

26. *Ex* meaning "of" or "from" and *periri* meaning "try" or "attempt."

27. Restaurant names cannot be expressed as interval or ratio scales (they are nominal variables) and the Rule of Five measures the median.

28. If it wasn't detectable, it wouldn't matter because it would have no consequence.

29. Answers may vary. Example answer: You shouldn't put a price on human life; however, sometimes choices have to be made if resources are limited, like whether to save the life of an older or a younger person. Also, the objection that measurement is somehow demeaning to humans is ironic since mathematics is as unique to humanity as language and art.

30. Answers may vary, but may include: Project costs cannot be extrapolated from historical experience because each project is unique. Or new product revenues cannot be estimated using historical data because each new product is unique.

31. A single randomly selected value from a population has a 50% chance of being above (or below) the median, based on the definition of a median.

For drawing several randomly selected values from a population, each will have a 50% chance of being above (or below) the median. The probability that all values are on one side of the median is the complement to the probability that the range of randomly selected values will include values on both sides of the median (so the probability of these events totals to 1).

Rule of...	P (all under the median)	P (all above the median)	P (all are above OR all below the median)	P (there is at least 1 value above the median and at least 1 value below the median)
X	0.5^X	0.5^X	0.5^X + 0.5^X	1 − (0.5^X + 0.5^X)
2	0.2500	0.2500	0.5000	0.5000
3	0.1250	0.1250	0.2500	0.7500
4	0.0625	0.0625	0.1250	0.8750
5	0.0313	0.0313	0.0625	0.9375
6	0.0156	0.0156	0.0313	0.9688
7	0.0078	0.0078	0.0156	0.9844
8	0.0039	0.0039	0.0078	0.9922
9	0.0020	0.0020	0.0039	0.9961
10	0.0010	0.0010	0.0020	0.9980

32. Answer will be open-ended but should identify a specific example and discuss how one of the four assumptions would have improved the measurement effort. Perhaps the measurement was avoided because it was simply presumed that no measurement like that had ever been done, that there wasn't enough data, and that large amounts of data were needed, and simply getting new data was not considered. Reversing any one of those assumptions could have resulted in at least attempting to measure the item in question.

CHAPTER 4

Clarifying the Measurement Problem

1. D
2. B
3. D
4. D
5. False. The relevance of any measurement, including greenhouse gas emissions, is that it might lead to better actions.
6. True. Without specifically identified decisions, the manager is merely hoping that the measurement will be informative in some valuable way—which is no better than not having any decision in mind. Only with a specific decision or set of decisions identified can we compute how the uncertainty of that variable affects the decision.
7. True, although this particular decision model has avoidable flaws that must be addressed.
8. C
9. False
10. C
11. B. The alternative of not having worker safety is not a feasible alternative. A feasible alternative is whether or not a particular safety program is justified.
12. E
13. True
14. False. For example, actuarial science in the insurance industry measures uncertainty and risk routinely.
15. C

16. False. Since neither outcome indicates a loss or negative conse-
    quence, this example of uncertainty is not an example of risk.

17. True

18. D

19. False. The insurance industry and others had practical definitions of
    these terms in the nineteenth century.

20. D

21. B

22. D

23. B

24. There is a risk that the need to act will be too subtle to be immedi-
    ately and consistently detected among the combination of variables
    on the dashboard. Another risk is that the manager will waste time
    deciding what to do and designing a specific response when the
    contingency could have been worked out in advance.

25. At least two of the following: unauthorized access by a hacker; theft
    of a laptop; a data center being hit by a fire, flood, or tornado; virus
    attacks.

26. "Risks" are framed in terms of outcomes involving loss, whereas
    "uncertainty" means that an outcome is merely unknown.

27. Both indicate a goal of a reduction in the risk of some future nega-
    tive consequence. In order to measure these, risk and risk reduction
    have to be measured.

28. D

CHAPTER 5

Calibrated Estimates: How Much Do You Know *Now?*

1. B
2. False. This represents your uncertainty about the bugs, not the actual average number of bugs.
3. False. Since we are focused on decision analysis, we require the subjective, Bayesian interpretation of probability. Under the frequentist's interpretation, probability cannot be applied to future, one-off events.
4. A
5. D
6. 50%
7. True. Being lucky enough to get 9 out of 10 is far more likely than being lucky enough to get 90 out of 100 if a person actually has a much less than 90% chance of the answers between their stated bounds.
8. False. While based on trivia questions, calibration exercises are really a measure of how well people evaluate their own uncertainty as opposed to how much they know about trivia.
9. A
10. C
11. C
12. True
13. B. De Finetti used the market price of a contract that would have a chance of paying a given amount as the "operational" definition of probability.
14. A
15. B

16. D

17. True

18. False

19. B

20. D

21. A

22. True. The research conducted by the author shows that after training with trivia questions, analysts were better at applying probabilities to predictions about real-world events than executives who have not had the training.

23. B. The frequency of seemingly calibrated results on 10 question tests is almost the same as the proportion of individuals from an uncalibrated population getting lucky with the test.

24. When the person claims to be 100% confident, every one of such responses must turn out to be correct or the person is overconfident.

25. A. The answer B contradicts the observed results, and the fact that analysts didn't get a higher number of questions right (they were only more realistic at assessing their uncertainties) indicates a lack of a clear knowledge advantage on the topic.

26. C

27. It establishes a base level of knowledge (we know something about a measurement) and provides guidance on how we should measure it or even whether we should measure it. It is the basis of computing the value of additional information.

CHAPTER 6

Quantifying Risk through Modeling

1. True
2. B
3. A
4. A
5. B
6. C
7. C
8. A
9. B
10. With the mean equal to (80 + 160)/2 and the standard deviation equal to (160 − 80)/3.29 the formula would be = norminv(rand(), (80 + 160)/2, (160 − 80)/3.29)
11. False. The bounds of a 90% CI are 1.645 standard deviations from the mean.
12. C
13. D
14. A. Set up a spreadsheet like the following to do the Monte Carlo simulation.

A	B	C	D	E
Scenario	Year 1 Cash in	Value of Grant Funds Received	Year 1 Revenue	Year 1 Net Cash
	=-NORMINV (RAND(),2550000, (4000000 – 1100000)/3.29))	= IF(RAND()<=0.5, RAND() * (500000 – 200000) + 200000,0)	= NORMINV (RAND(),3300000, (4800000 – 1800000)/3.29)	Sum of B, C and D
1	($1,436,467)	$0	$2,746,892	$1,310,424
2	($1,274,807)	$0	$2,684,247	$1,409,440
3	($1,786,674)	$740,875	$4,287,420	$3,241,622
...	(Note that these are negative values in this column)	...	...	...
	Continue for at least a few thousand scenarios (e.g., 10,000)			

Summary Measure	Formula (Assume we are using 10,000 rows in the spreadsheet columns shown in the table above)	Value
Count of scenarios	=COUNTA(A4:A10003)	10,000
Count of scenarios with net cash <= –$1MM	=COUNTIF(E4 :E10003,"<=-1000000")	570
% Chance of Losing $1MM or more	570/10,000	**5.7%**

15. 34.38%

This could be approximated with a Monte Carlo simulation but this also has a simple algebraic solution. If only project A closes, then with its stated uniform distribution of $1 million to $2 million, there is a 75% chance of falling short of $1.5 million. If only project B closes ($1 million to $3 million), then there is a 50% chance of falling short. If both projects close, then the required $1.5 million is met since the minimum revenue would then be $2 million. So now we work out the chance of not meeting the required sales in each of the three situations where we can fall short: winning only A, winning only B, and winning neither. The values work out as shown below. If a Monte Carlo simulation is used, the answer should still be close to 34%.

Ways that less than $1.5MM can be made:		
Neither prospect closes	$(1 - .75) \times (1 - .5)$	0.125
Only A closes and is less than $1.5MM	$.75 \times (1 - .5) \times .5$	0.1875
Only B closes and is less than $1.5MM	$(1 - .75) \times (.5) \times .25$	0.03125
Total		0.34375

16. B
17. C
18. D
19. E
20. True
21. False. Taleb has criticized many mathematical models used in the financial industry but he himself is a Monte Carlo user.
22. 57 to 93. The range errors are +/−10 and +/−15. Take the square root of the sum of the squares of these errors; $(10^2 + 15^2)^{.5}. = 18$. The sum of the means is $30 + 45 = 75$. The range of the total is 75 +/−18.
23. "Low" and "medium" aren't quantified and are therefore ambiguous.
24. At least two of the following: analyst certification; calibrator certification; procedures and templates for calibrator input; use of a single tool set.
25. Companies tend to use quantitative analysis for routine operations, rather than for larger and more important considerations. An example is that of using Monte Carlo simulations for routine production operations instead of for major IT projects or strategic decisions.
26. The responses should include at least three of the following Monte Carlo tools: AIE Wizard, @Risk, Crystal Ball, Risk Solver, XLSim, Analytica, SAS, IBM SPSS Statistics, Mathematica, ModelRisk, RiskAmp, R.
27. Set up a table in Excel similar to the one that follows. Formulas are shown in the row indicated. Create the formula, then drag down until the number of rows is equal to the number of Monte Carlo trials.

    To find the percentage of scenarios that are at least two hours late, add up the relative frequencies from the bins that are six hours and above in the relative frequency table. **The answer should be close to 20%.**

    Download the complete spreadsheet example for this and other spreadsheet problems at www.howtomeasureanything.com.

B	C	D	E	F	G	H	I	J	K	L	M	N	O
Scenario	Prob of Weather Occurrence	Weather Event Occurrence Random Variable Test	Weather Risk in Effect	Outcome of Weather Delay (Hours)	Effective Weather Delay	Prob of Road Const	Road Const Occurrence Random Variable Test	Road Const Risk in Effect	Outcome of Road Const Risk (Hours)	Effective Road Const Delay	Total Delay (Hours)	Non-Delay Portion of Delivery Outcome (Hours)	Total Delivery Time (Hours)
Formula	= 0.1	= RAND()	= IF(D2 <C2, 1, 0)	= NORMINV (RAND(), (5−0.5)/2, (5−0.5)/ 3.29)	= E2 × F2	= 0.15	= Rand()	= IF(I2<= H2,1,0)	= RAND() × (5 − 2) + 2	= J2 × K2	= G2 + L2	= NORMINV (RAND(), (3.5 + 4.25)/2, (4.25 − 3.5)/ 3.29)	= M2 + N2
1	0.100	0.099	1.000	4.656	4.656	0.150	0.288	0.000	3.188	0.000	4.656	3.960	8.616
2	0.100	0.107	0.000	1.468	0.000	0.150	0.935	0.000	3.946	0.000	0.000	3.895	3.895
3	0.100	0.398	0.000	1.375	0.000	0.150	0.657	0.000	2.191	0.000	0.000	3.914	3.914
...	...	...	...	...	...	...	...	...	...	...	...	...	...
10,000	0.100	0.749	0.000	4.102	0.000	0.150	0.273	0.000	2.346	0.000	0.000	3.591	3.591

Q	R	S
Upper Limit of Bin (Hours)	Frequency	Relative Frequency
=2	{=FREQUENCY(O2:O10001,Q2:Q42)}	=R2/SUM($R$2:$R$42)
2.00	1	0.0100%
2.01	0	0.0000%
2.02	0	0.0000%
...	...	...
12	0	0.0000%

Quantifying the Value of Information

1. A
2. B
3. C
4. C
5. E
6. True
7. B
8. A threshold is the exact value an uncertain variable on a continuum would have in order to break even on a decision. Below that value one choice is better and above that value another choice is better.
9. A

   Threshold = 6 × X = 3,000,000
   Solving for X, X = 500,000
   Relative threshold = (500,000 – 300,000)/(800,000 – 300,000) = 0.4
   EOLF (using EOLF chart) = 80
   EVPI = EOLF/1,000 × OL per unit × (BB – WB) = 240,000

   Or the spreadsheet for information value for normal distributions can be used to produce a value that should be close to the same.
10. E
11. A
12. D
13. True
14. E
15. C
16. A

17. B

18. E

19. 16%

Using the Excel function we write: =NORMDIST(85,100,15,1)

20. $20,000

EOL = .2 × $100,000 = $20,000

21. 0.33

RT = (Threshold − WB)/(BB − WB)
=(6000 − 4000)/(10000 − 4000)

22. Using either the EOLF chart or the information value for normal distributions, you should get an answer close to about $17,000 or so.

23. A situation where demand is uncertain but the losses from overstocking are less than the losses for understocking by the same amount.

24.

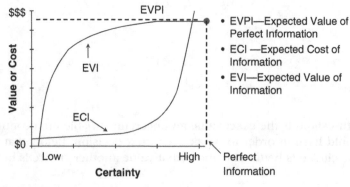

- EVPI—Expected Value of Perfect Information
- ECI —Expected Cost of Information
- EVI—Expected Value of Information

25. Challenge:

    1. The discrete approximation starts with creating a table that divides the distribution into a large number of increments—perhaps hundreds or perhaps even one increment per unit of the product.

    2. For each increment, compute the probability of that increment given the 90% CI entered.

    3. For each increment, compute a loss of either overstocking or understocking using the formula =ABS(X − 1500) × L (or any expression that produces the same result) where X refers to the number of units in the increment and L is the loss per unit entered (Note: The =ABS() function is simply taking the absolute value of the difference so that negative numbers are turned into positive numbers—which is correct given that the loss is the same in both directions in this case. An =if() statement could be constructed to produce the same result.)

4. Multiply the incremental probability by the loss of an increment and add up the products to get EVPI.

Changing the entered 90% CI and loss per unit in your spreadsheet should, of course, change the EPVI. To test your spreadsheet, enter a 90% CI of 1,000 to 2,000 and a loss per unit of $10 if understocked or overstocked. The EVPI should be about $2,400 (answers will vary a bit depending on choices like increment size, but the answer should not vary by more than 10%).

CHAPTER 8

The Transition: From What to Measure to How to Measure

1. D
2. D
3. False
4. B
5. True
6. B
7. True
8. Answers should include terms like "standard deviation," "survey of companies," "correlation," or "experiment" combined with the search term of interest like "sales training" and "increased sales."
9. D
10. False
11. A
12. B
13. True
14. True
15. B
16. B
17. Answers will vary but may include: number of employees of different types, and time spent in different unproductive activities by type of employee. The example should show how the decomposed values are used to compute total unproductive time.
18. At least three of the following: decompose the measurement so that it can be estimated from other measurements; consider your findings from secondary research; place one or more of the elements from

the decomposition in one or more of the methods of observation (trails left behind, direct observation, tracking with "tags," or experiments); keep the concept of "just enough" squarely in mind; think about the errors specific to that problem.

19. "Empirical" refers to the use of observation as evidence for a conclusion.

20. At least two of the following: it's been done before—don't reinvent the wheel; you have access to more data than you think—it might just involve some resourceful use of what you have; you need less data than you think—if you are clever about how to analyze it; an adequate amount of new data is probably more accessible than you first thought.

21. The response should mention that all empirical methods have some error, so spending the full EVPI is not justified. Also, initial measurements often change the value of continued measurement. Finally, the information value curve is usually steepest at the beginning while the cost of information rises slowly. So the biggest uncertainty reduction tends to be early in a measurement, anyway.

22. That the sheer size of the sample could "average out" systematic error.

CHAPTER 9

Sampling Reality: How Observing Some Things Tells Us about All Things

1. B
2. False. You should narrow it.
3. True
4. A
5. A
6. False
7. E
8. A
9. B
10. True
11. A
12. C
13. D
    Upper Bound on Chart = about 2
    Lower Bound on Chart = about 0.075
    Max Serial Number − Min Serial Number = 10107348 − 10085197 = 22,151
    Upper Bound Estimate = 22,151 × (1 + 2) = 66,453
    Lower Bound Estimate = 22,151 × (1 + .075) = 23,812
14. B
15. C

16. A

The variance is equal to the square of the standard deviation.
Divide the sample variance by the number in each sample:
$3,000^2/40 = 225,000$
$3,041.38^2/70 = 132,142.86$
Add the two from above:
$225,000 + 132,142.86 = 357,142.86$
Find the square root of the result:
Sqrt(357,142.86) = 597.61
Compute the difference of sample means:
$35,000 - 34,000 = 1,000$
Chance that the mean revenue produced by extroverts is lower than
that of nonextroverts = Normdist(0, 1000, 597.61, 1) = 4.7%

17. A

18. B

19. A. Recall that a negative correlation is not the same as weakly correlated. It means that as one variable increases, the other decreases. A
correlation of $-.98$ means that when one variable increases the other
decreases in a highly predictable way.

20. C

21. True

22. Sample Mean (point estimate) = $(70 + 73 + 75 + 71 + 80)/5 = 73.8$
Standard error of the estimate of the mean =SQRT(VAR
$(70,73,75,71,80)/5)\wedge.5 = 1.772$
$t = 2.13$ (given)
90% CI for Mean = Point Estimate $\pm t \times$ Stdev
90% CI for Mean = $73.8 \pm 2.13 \times 1.77 = 70$ to 77.6

23. $936 - 1,587$
Stdev of Proportion = Sqrt(P $\times$ (1 $-$ P))
Proportion Tagged = $34/200 = 0.17$
Stdev of Proportion Tagged = Sqrt(0.17 $\times$ (1-0.17)) = 0.0266
$z = 1.645$
90% CI for the Proportion Tagged = $0.17 \pm z \times$ Stdev
= $0.17 \pm 1.645 \times 0.0266$
= .126 to .2137
In terms of the number of wekas in the population, these propor-
tions imply a 90% CI of
$200/.2137$ to $200/.126$
= 936 to 1,587

24. 29% – 63%

Use Exhibit 9.5, Population Proportion 90% CI for Small Samples, or the Population Proportion spreadsheet from the Chapter 9 downloads.

25. It's known as a controlled experiment. The test group is manipulated in some way and the control group is not.

26. 1

To use an Excel spreadsheet, you may enter, for example, series X into the first 10 rows of column A, enter series Y in the first 10 rows of column B, and write the Excel function =correl(B1:B10,A1:A10).

27. Correlation = 0.61.

Enter the data into a spreadsheet in a manner similar to what is shown in answer 26 earlier and write the Excel function =correl(clients acquired, sales calls).

28. If C calls are made, then the number of clients acquired predicted by the regression equation is:

Clients Acquired = 0.0705 × C + 4.7983

Entering data into a spreadsheet as in answer 27, write Excel functions: =slope(clients acquired, sales calls) and =intercept(clients acquired, sales calls).

CHAPTER 10

Bayes: Adding to What You Know Now

1. C
2. True
3. False
4. False
5. A
6. True
7. B
8. True
9. B
10. True
11. A
12. D
13. C
14. They are not internally consistent.
    P(M)P(P|M) + P(~M)P(P|~M) = (.7 × .5) + (.3 × .8) = .59
    instead of .85
15. 63.3%
    P(H)P(TP|H)/P(TP) = .5 (.95/.75) = .633
16. P(Democrat|Urban) = P(Democrat) × P(Urban|Democrat) / P(Urban)
17. It does constitute evidence that the spouse is not cheating on him (absence of evidence is, in fact, evidence, but not proof of absence).
18. (0.05 × 0.8) + (0.5 × 0.6) = 70%
19. Use impartial judges if possible; use blinds when possible; use separation of duties; precommit to Bayesian consequences.

20. 13%, = BINOMDIST(5, 20, 1/6, 0)

21. 8%, =normdist(.7,(.75 + .3)/2,(.75 − .3)/3.29,1)-
normdist(.65,(.75 + .3)/2,(.75 − .3)/3.29,1)

The mean of the confidence interval of 30% to 75% is 52.5%.

The standard deviation is given by the range between the upper and lower bound of the 90% CI, and the fact that the lower and upper bounds are 3.29 standard deviations apart.

Standard Deviation = (75% − 30)/3.29 = 13.68%

Compute the difference between the cumulative normal distribution going from 70% to 65%.

NORMDIST(0.70,0.525,0.1368,1) − NORMDIST(0.65,0.525,0.1368,1) = 8%

22. 50.3% − 73.7%

23. From Bayes' rule we can write P(Disease|Positive test) = P(Disease) × P(Positive test|Disease)/P(Positive test).

Use Rule 4 to rewrite P(Positive test) from the denominator of the right-hand side of the above equation: P(Positive test) = P(Positive test|Disease) × P(Disease) + P(Positive test|~Disease) × P(~Disease). Then substitute in values from the problem statement:

(1/100,000) × 0.95 / [(1/100,000) × 0.95 + 0.005 × (99,999/100,000)] = 0.0019 = 0.19%

24. The probability that touch therapy works would represent the prior probability.

Preference and Attitudes:
The Softer Side of Measurement

1. True
2. A
3. D
4. True
5. D
6. C
7. E
8. D
9. C
10. A
11. False
12. B
13. E
14. Response Set X
15. B
16. A
17. C
18. A
19. A
20. False
21. D
22. True
23. D
24. B

25. A

26. B

27. False

28. If they really thought a human life was priceless, they would forego every luxury and devote all time and wealth to saving whatever lives they could. Invariably, they do not.

29. $25,000

30. He believes that these factors are outside of management's control.

CHAPTER 12

The Ultimate Measurement Instrument: Human Judges

1. D
2. A
3. C
4. False. He found no correlation.
5. B
6. A
7. C
8. True
9. C
10. A
11. False
12. E
13. False. They merely reduce inconsistency error of experts. They are generally inferior to models based on objective historical data.
14. A
15. B
16. E
17. False
18. B
19. A
20. $=\ln(0.4/0.6) = -0.405$
21. 50%; in Excel you can write =1/(1/exp(0)+1).

CHAPTER 13

New Measurement Instruments for Management

1. D
2. C
3. False. He was able to beat them.
4. True
5. C
6. C
7. B
8. A
9. B
10. D
11. A
12. False
13. D
14. GPS Insight combines GPS, wireless networks, Internet access, and Google Earth.
15. Social science research used to rely heavily on self-reported surveys that have turned out to be highly inconsistent with what objective location tracking data says.
16. He used data about the use of search terms from Google users in different geographic locations and correlated searches for terms like "flu symptoms" with actual flu outbreaks.
17. Refer to the author's "surf, friend, say, go, buy, and play" taxonomy. Specifically: (1) what we search on search engines and websites we go to, (2) our connections on social networks, (3) what we say on blogs and microblogs, (4) our locations and movements, (5) what we buy on the Internet, and (6) how we play.

18. Screen-scrapers can bog down a site's performance. Websites like eBay and Facebook provide developers with APIs that give developers direct access to large amounts of data in a way that the service provider can control.

19. Their clients were less happy after a trip than before it, so they retrained the sales team to better focus on customer experience and measured the results.

20. At least two of the following: sleep disorders, depression, physical health, alcohol use, happiness, or others listed in the book.

21. At least two of the following: unemployment, retail sales, travel, flu outbreaks, or other items mentioned in the book.

22. The outcomes of predictions can be tracked over time and are well-calibrated. The prices of the prediction securities at various times compare well to the eventual outcomes. For example, of prediction securities that sell at 20 cents on the dollar, about 20% should come true.

CHAPTER 14

A Universal Measurement Method: Applied Information Economics

1. B
2. Identify experts; plan workshops; conduct initial research.
3. Decision problem definition; decision model detail; initial calibrated estimates.
4. Value of information analysis; preliminary measurement method designs; measurements methods; updated decision model; final value of information analysis.
5. Completed risk/return analysis; identified metrics procedures; decision optimization; final report and presentation.
6. C
7. A
8. C
9. C
10. B
11. True
12. True
13. False
14. False
15. No, most of the uncertainties about things like state adoption rates of the technology, efficiency improvements, and improved reporting rates turned out to have an information value of 0. Only a few variables had a significant information value.
16. They identified five possible categories of benefits: lower cost per transaction, lower error rates, reusability of code, faster implementations, and improved business intelligence. Since the change

in delivery time and cost of projects had a high information value, more in-depth data gathering was done to reduce uncertainty about how standards affect project duration.

For questions 17 to 19, students are encouraged to go into more detail than provided here. Answers should be graded by whether they are detailed enough to actually facilitate modeling of the problem. This could be the basis of a more extensive paper on the topic of choice. Basic examples are provided here only as a seed for further development.

17. Examples: You are trying to decide which faculty member should be granted tenure. Or you are trying to determine if an increase in R&D spending is justified. Or you are trying to determine if new leadership or new policies will improve the chance of creating successful products.

18. Example: You might attempt to determine the number of times they've been cited by other authors and determine how this affects institutional objectives, like increased grants, alumni donations, or enrollment, if those were the objectives. You could forecast future product success based on characteristics that indicate success.

19. You could use this as one consideration in a measure of faculty productivity, including how often their work is cited. This might be part of a measurement to support decisions about granting tenure.

20. Improved availability of information could mean you spend less time looking for information and you lose it less often. To get started, the average duration of document searching, the frequency of document re-creation, and the frequency of going without (per year) are quantities calibrated estimators can put ranges on.

21. Responses could include any of the following examples or other equally detailed responses. Flexibility might mean how quickly equipment could be changed to produce new goods. The rate that new products are created could be considered, and savings in equipment switchover can be estimated. Or perhaps flexibility means the equipment could produce a wider array of products. Estimations of the markets for the other categories of products that currently cannot be produced would be modeled. Or perhaps flexibility means that the equipment works with standard parts, making repairs faster and cheaper.

22. The assumption that market volatility is normally distributed.

23.

1. If it's really that important, it's something you can define. If it's something you think exists at all, it's something you've already observed somehow.

2. If it's something important and something uncertain, you have a cost of being wrong and a chance of being wrong.

3. You can quantify your current uncertainty with calibrated estimates.

4. You can compute the value of additional information by knowing the "threshold" of the measurement where it begins to make a difference compared to your existing uncertainty.

5. Once you know what it is worth to measure something, you can put the measurement effort in context and decide on the effort it should take.

6. Knowing just a few methods for random sampling, controlled experiments, Bayesian methods, or even merely improving on the judgments of experts can lead to a significant reduction in uncertainty.